PRAISE FOR *LIVING REAL*

"Camille has created a bold pathway through the discomfort, hard truths, and fear of vulnerability that can keep us disconnected from our most true selves and meaningful lives we crave."

—Karen Finney, Strategic Communications

"From awareness about the "lies we've been sold," to embracing discomfort, to holding multiple truths at once, Preston offers a playbook for how to engage deeply with the world. Her book provides a practice for your internal compass that will inform your role as a leader—of yourself, your family, and your team/organization. Read it today and start to finally live Real"

—Joey Coleman, international keynote speaker and WSJ best-selling author of *Never Lose an Employee Again*

"*Living Real* is a compassionate, practical guide for anyone feeling emotionally adrift in today's hyper-connected world. Camille Preston's honest and heartfelt approach encourages readers to reconnect with themselves, embrace life's full spectrum of emotions, and redefine success through authenticity, depth, and presence. Highly recommended for genuine, transformative living."

—Andrew Smith, Founder, Blue Rose

"In a world that rushes us past pain and numbs emotion, *Living Real* invites us to slow down, feel fully, and engage more deeply. Camille reminds us that grief and discomfort are gateways to growth, clarity, and connection. This book is a call to stop hiding from the hard emotions and to start living more fully by embracing what is, in all its rawness and beauty."

—Christina Luconi, CPO, Rapid7

"There are real benefits of Realing — but you have to be willing to dig deep and engage yourself in this work. This book digs in at a specifically unsettling time and I would recommend it to anyone looking to make meaning in what too often feels like an upside-down world. You will walk away from it feeling you are truly seeing things right-side up for the first time."

—Andrew Coy, CEO, Digital Harbor Foundation

"In her new book, Camille Preston offers profound insights into navigating life's many challenges. Her personal experiences as well as her years of professional work bring a sense of compassion and understanding to wide-ranging reflections on grief, parenting, and conflict. She underscores that we are all under personal, societal, and spiritual stress, and gives us a new perspective on recognizing this reality. This book is not about coping or managing; it shows you why it is critical to understand the reality of the pain and to set your emotions free, allowing your innate strength to develop, grow, and flourish. In telling her own stories, she provides context to yours and shows you how your power can and will prevail."

—Linda Watt, Retired Ambassador

"*Living Real* strips away the illusion that operational excellence has to come at the cost of personal well-being. Camille speaks directly to the overextended professionals who've built a life of achievement—and quietly wonder why it still doesn't feel like enough. This book is a smart, introspective guide for recalibrating success from the inside out."

—Diane Danielson, COO Matmarket, LLC

"*Living Real* is the kind of book you give to someone who's ready for their next chapter. It's more than a read—it's a reframe. Camille's work is steeped in the kind of clarity only lived experience can offer."

—Christine Sperber,
Co-Founder Modern Elder Academy

"High-performing professionals often delay the inner work until something breaks. Camille's book gives you a smarter path. *Living Real* reframes success so that it includes not excludes presence, perspective, and peace of mind."

—Catherine Allen, CEO, The Santa Fe Group and Founder, Board Risk Committee

"Camille Preston is a brilliant business psychologist with the heart and head to see the trappings of our modern working lives. Vital, relevant, and expressed with poetic knowing of emotion and expertise, *Living Real* shares her deeply felt wisdom and gives us permission and tools to experience life anew, so our souls can calm and soar."

—Joanne Gordon, author of *Be Happy at Work*

"Caregiving, career, motherhood, expectations—we carry all of it. *Living Real* doesn't ask you to drop the weight. It asks you to stop carrying it alone. It's powerful, personal, and long overdue."

—Liz O'Donnell, Founder, Working Daughters

"In *Living Real*, organizational psychologist Dr. Camille Preston provides a compassionate framework that helps people move beyond societal metrics of outer success to cultivating inner awareness, authenticity, and courage which can lead to a more vibrant, meaningful, and sustainable life."

—Victoria Maizes MD, Founding Executive Director, Andrew Weil Center for Integrative Medicine and author

"Whether tackling grief, internal or external obstacles, or navigating personal passions and professional ambitions, a leader in a moment of decision and transition will find Preston's ability to make clear what can be chaotic. A powerful read."

—Susan King, Dean Emeritus, UNC Hussman School of Journalism & Media

"This book doesn't ask you to start over. It asks you to start being honest—with yourself. *Living Real* is strong, clear, and unapologetically true."

—Cappy Daume, Chief Portfolio Management Officer, The Davis Companies

"In *Living Real*, Dr. Camille Preston takes the reader on a journey through the obstacles that many of us face in expressing ourselves authentically. Highlighting how difficulties in our lives are often the springboard into finding deeper truths, she encourages the reader to move beyond the impediments of the stress and pace of the modern world. Dr. Preston's background in psychology, leadership coaching and tenacious personal development work lends itself to her use of both narrative and principles of personal change to make her message simple for those that are seeking a simple, meaningful change in how they approach their professional and personal lives."

—Ann Marie Chiasson MD, MPH, University of Arizona, Andrew Weil Center for Integrative Medicine

"In a world that rewards emotional repression, Camille offers a path of tenderness, truth, and transformation. *Living Real* invites you to exhale, giving voice to the grief and disconnection we often carry in silence. This book doesn't fix you; it frees you. Camille's honesty meets you with compassion, wisdom, and an unwavering belief in your wholeness."

—Erika Boissiere,
Founder & MFT, The Relationship Therapy Group

"Reading *Living Real* is like sharing stories about what really matters in life with a trusted and wise friend. Camille will inspire you to be both courageous and vulnerable in discerning the challenges and bloopers of life with honesty and candidness. She will encourage you to question and be more curious about the depths of how you truly feel and less a spectator to your own existence. If you long to be less distracted by the leadership pressure to conform this world, and desire a life transformed through the discovery of personal joy, read this book!"

— Dr. William H. Morley, MBA, BCC,
President, ExCL Group

"*Living Real* is a timely call-to-action. Busy people everywhere will recognize themselves in its reflections on our overstretched lives. Drawing on decades of coaching experience, Camille Preston offers an antidote—an opportunity to shift from constant striving to a life rooted in authenticity and presence. A gift of wisdom to be savored."

— Carol Van Den Hende, American Fiction Award-winning author of the *Goodbye Orchid* series

"As a psychologist and coach, I have seen how much energy people spend holding it together. Camille speaks to that silent fatigue. *Living Real* offers a path that's honest, restorative, and long overdue."

— William Courville, PhD,
Founder, Courville Consulting

LIVING
REAL

LIVING
REAL

LIVING REAL

Redefining Success, Presence, and Happiness

Camille Preston, PhD

Living Real
© 2025 Camille Preston

All rights reserved. No part of this book may be reproduced or transmitted in any form or by any means, electronic or mechanical, including photocopying, recording, or by any information storage and retrieval system, without written permission from the author. Published by AIM Leadership. For publishing enquiries contact AIMleadership.com

The information provided within this book is for general informational purposes only. The author is not a mental health or medical professional offering advice in that capacity. Although every effort has been made to ensure that information in this book was correct at press time, the author does not assume, and hereby disclaims, any liability to any party for any loss, damage, or disruption caused by errors or omissions, whether such errors or omissions result from negligence, accident, or any other cause.

NO AI TRAINING: Without in any way limiting the author's and publisher's exclusive rights under copyright, any use of this publication to "train" generative artificial intelligence (AI) technologies to generate text is expressly prohibited. The author reserves all rights to license uses of this work for generative AI training and development of machine learning language models.

Cover Design: James T. Egan, bookflydesign.com
Illustrations: Kevin Newhall, kevinnewhall.carbonmade.com
Interior Design: Amit Dey, amitdey2528@gmail.com
Publishing Consultant: Geoff Affleck, authorpreneurbooks.com
Audiobook Engineer: David Porter, mixonestudios.com

ISBN 978-0-9849041-3-6 (paperback)
ISBN 978-0-9849041-5-0 (hardcover)
ISBN 978-0-9849041-4-3 (eBook)
ISBN 978-0-9849041-6-7 (audiobook)

To those who've shared this path to Living Real—
You know who you are.

And, to Mark, Adie and Pres—
You are my *M.A.P* of what matters.

INVITATION TO ACTION

Make the Most of What You Read

A great book doesn't just inform—it transforms. But transformation only happens when insights become action. That's why we've created a set of simple, practical tools to help you *reflect*, *integrate*, and *apply* what you've learned in each chapter.

Whether you're flipping back through a section or moving full speed ahead, these bite-sized activities are designed to make behavior change happen—without overwhelm or overthinking.

And because life doesn't pause when inspiration strikes, we've also built an app that lets you capture your insights, track your growth, and stay engaged on the go.

Visit LivingReal.AIMleadership.com/activities or scan the QR code to get started.

Contents

Introduction: The Call to Live Real   1

PART I : The Problem of Shallowing   **15**
  1 The Curse of the Shallows   17
  2 The Lies We Were Sold   47
  3 Costs of Living Disconnected   71
  4 An Invitation to Real   91

PART II: The Opportunity to Real   **105**
  5 Embracing Both/And   109
  6 Break the Cycle   127
  7 Hold The Tension   147
  8 Connect More Deeply   163

PART III: A Guide for Living Real — 175
   9 Build Our Inner Capacity — 177
   10 Learn to Listen Inwardly — 195
   11 Engage Depth — 205
   12 Create Space for Presence — 215

Conclusion: Coming Alive — 237

Further Reading + Bonus Resources — 241

Acknowledgements — 243

About the Author — 245

Appendix: Definitions — 247

Introduction

THE CALL TO LIVE REAL

We live in a world that rushes us past negative emotions. That asks us to swallow our pain. That tells us to keep focused forward until we feel *fine*, even when we are anything but okay. We quickly learn that sorrow is to be managed, shortened, and silenced. Even when we give hard feelings space, it is with the goal of moving on more quickly. We talk about "moving on" as if life were a race and emotions, something to avoid and leave behind, when the exact opposite is true.

We are overextended and exhausted. We are living in a world that is more digitally connected than ever, yet less genuinely connected to one another. We live next to neighbors we never meet, and work in places where we rarely see others. Not surprisingly, we are living at the height of a mental health epidemic. This is exacerbated by years of buying into illusions of happiness and hiding from hard feelings behind social media posts. But the feelings do not go away. What we do not allow ourselves to be with, we do not metabolize, nor can we use to propel us towards growth.

Grief is all around us and comes in many different forms. Too often, we think of grief as being only about death. But grief can arise anytime we lose something that matters to us or face any number of difficult moments. You can grieve the end of a friendship, a change in your health, when jobs disappear, or when hopes do not pan out. Even expected changes, like kids growing up or moving out, can cause grief.

I propose to you that these difficult moments in our lives, these times of sorrow and grief, are not something to just "get over" but something to move through. When held with presence and reverence, challenges and experiences can open and expand us rather than diminish us. But in order to do that, it's crucial to build our capacity to be present, to hold the tension, and to experience all of the complex emotions that are so very vital to living fully and thriving.

Living Real is an invitation for you to do all of that. To experience the full range of your humanity. To reconnect with and allow all of your emotions, uncensored and unprotected, in all of their messy, raw beauty. To remove what is distracting or no longer aligned. It is an invitation to move into a deeper, fuller presence.

This book is intended to help you step out of a simplified existence, one that I refer to as "Shallowed," so that you can retrieve the parts of yourself that have been tucked away in the basement of your psyche. I am inviting you—and giving you the tools—to feel not just the easy feelings but all of them. To be fully alive, to be fully human, is to hold both joy and sorrow, light and dark, hope and heartbreak.

This book is for anyone who has ever gone numb and longed to feel again. For anyone who has achieved all they were told to chase yet found themselves Shallowed. For anyone who has ever known profound loss and wondered how to keep going. For anyone navigating adversity and craving a safe space to be truly genuine. For anyone wondering, "Is this it?"

We do not aspire to go through challenging moments in life. But we need to. If we face them with rigor and vulnerability, and if we allow ourselves to be with the complex emotions rather than rushing to leave them behind, we can begin to live more authentically. The question is not whether life will break you—it will. The question is whether or not you allow life's challenges to break you open into an even better version of yourself.

The opposite of a Shallowed existence is when we Real. Yes, that is a verb. My own need to Real came after navigating a season of grief—five deaths in five months. During that time, I craved being with people who were willing to be with me just as I was. I sought out people unfazed when tears and laughter erupted, often in the same moment. Those who sugarcoated the complexity or retreated into politically correct niceties felt vapid.

As I became more fully present with my emotional loss, I grew acutely aware of the sorrow living within all of us and how we have lost our ability to actually feel hard or uncomfortable emotions. In losing that, we have lost something even greater: our ability to experience the depth of our human existence.

I was inspired to write this book after realizing how many people around me were struggling to have hard conversations or were grappling with how to be present enough to cope with life's more challenging experiences. Transitions, whether a loss, change, or still point, bring space for perspective and more conscious choices.

Even when these transitions are anticipated, *good*, or coveted, they can present challenges. For example, becoming an empty nester or a retiree creates a still point—space to wrestle with bigger, more personal questions. Sometimes, transitions are involuntary, creating forced periods of reflection, such as a termination, illness, or diagnosis. Sometimes, they are more mundane, like the lifelong runner forced to give up her passion due to an injury.

Our discomfort with stillness and being Real stems from years of hiding from hard feelings and buying into illusions of happiness. What we do not allow ourselves to be with, we do not metabolize. In Chapter 3, we will explore how this is contributing to the mental health pandemic.

A friend once said to me, "My dad was old, lonely, and really unwell. So why am I so sad that he died?" I credit my season of grief for helping me to recognize that what my friend needed at that moment was to be Real. Instead of replying, I waited, giving him my full attention as he answered his own question. With his only living sibling incapacitated, he felt even more alone in the world. The death of his father was more than a death; he realized it felt like the end of his family as he knew it.

When he finished, his eyes welled up, and he simply said, "Thank you." For months, he struggled to understand why he felt such deep sorrow. His gratitude, he told me, was for being given the space to voice his loneliness, to surface the weight of emotions he had been carrying, and to be witnessed in his messiness. He found immediate relief simply by acknowledging what he was feeling rather than ignoring his emotions or just moving on without truly processing it.

What It Means to Live Real

Living Real invites you to strip away what does not serve you—anything that does not bring you a sense of aliveness. Whether these are internal stories you have told yourself or external metrics you've chased, these illusions are often the very constraints keeping you from living Real. When you shed other people's expectations, you break cycles that no longer serve. Realing becomes the practice of showing up to life fully without numbing, performing, or pulling back. It is the gateway to intentionally choosing the life you want to live.

Living Real beckons you to engage more deeply with all of life. It's about embracing who you are and becoming comfortable with the full spectrum of the human experience. When you welcome the full range of your own feelings, you'll no longer need to avoid adversity. That's because the tender, painful moments are as pivotal as the awe-inspiring ones as you reclaim inner ease, alignment, and vitality.

Living Real challenges you to be more fully present. To create safe spaces where challenging emotions can surface. To hold the complexity of emotions—the contrast between our ecstatic peaks and devastating valleys, between our celebrations and setbacks, between peace and despair.

Being with the tension that is naturally inherent in life—the both/and—creates space for new ways of thinking, feeling, and being. We will explore this concept in Chapter 5. When you can embrace contrasts, rather than running from them, we can grow from the inevitability of a life that is both/and. In turn, you will create space to hear your own more profound, more authentic understanding of what it means to be successful, to feel happiness, and to be you.

What if the path to Living Real was simple?

R—Remove what is misaligned, distracting, or no longer serving.

E—Engage more deeply.

A—Allow the full range of feelings.

L—Let yourself be even more fully present.

Living Real calls you to a more genuine, aligned, authentic version of you. A version of you that reconnects with what motivates you and what fulfills you. A *you* who cultivates a presence so profound that even ordinary moments become sacred. A you that brings your whole self to every aspect of your life in a way that inspires those around you. A more successful you.

The ability to live Real begins with what I call Realing.

> *[DEF] Realing: Being present and engaged in the full range of life. Being with and embracing all of what is—the raw, genuine, unfiltered. Feeling fully what is, in that moment, standing inside the ache, the joy, the not-yet-knowing, without Shallowing, negating, or numbing emotions away.*

Realing is not about abandoning who you are, minimizing your hard-earned success, or adding more to your already overflowing plate. It is about realizing a more integrated fulfillment and well-being, one that extends beyond simply *what* you accomplish. This is the success of thriving. It is being fully present and engaged while walking through each step of your daily life.

Living Real doesn't happen overnight. It takes courage to face what you've buried, wisdom to challenge what you've accepted, and compassion for the parts of yourself you've abandoned along the way. But I promise you this: A new kind of life awaits you on the other side of your Realing journey. A new life of such richness, depth, and vibrant aliveness that you will wonder how—and, importantly, why—you ever settled for less.

I've been deeply humbled by the response I've received to the concept of this book. Many have come to me stilled, silenced—with tears in their eyes, profoundly reminded of how many of us are struggling with grief, loss, loneliness, and despair, and seeking a path forward.

We are in tough times—politically, socially, economically, in a world full of loneliness, burnout, depression, and anxiety. We are suffering at the individual, family, and community levels. And there are so many feelings that we don't know how to feel, process, metabolize, or release. We default to repressing and dismissing these struggles, and it only makes these situations more difficult.

During the writing of this book, the world has been grieving on a global level. We live in a time when we are forced, at a rapid rate, to review all aspects of life, including wide-ranging changes in employment, societal norms, and programs that have historically brought safety and a voice to the unheard. We desperately need something to anchor us, which means taking an honest look at how Shallow our experiences have become. We must get Real with one another. We can no longer afford to live an Instagram life. We need to become comfortable with the tension of the uncomfortable and use it to embrace a fuller, more empowering life.

While the concepts in this book are applicable on many levels, I hope you'll embrace living Real in a personal way that will give you the presence, energy, and capacity to serve those around you. Just as we are reminded to put on our own oxygen mask before helping others, living Real yourself will give you the reverse you need to help someone else.

A grieving man once said to me, "I'm sick of people giving me books. I don't want to read books that make me feel worse by telling me how to feel better. I want to be in my grief, feeling heartbreak and sadness, AND in my joy again."

That is what Realing is all about. That's the kind of book I've tried to write. One that gives you hope at the end of the day. My goal with this book is to help you see how invaluable challenging experiences can be. How the very hard things we might have avoided can crack us open to new ways of living, new ways of feeling, new ways of being out in the world. Try thinking of Realing like the Japanese art of kintsugi. In this ancient tradition, when a teacup breaks, its cracks are filled with gold, not to hide the damage but to honor it and embrace it as part of the story.

It is an apt way to think about the negative experiences that break or interrupt our lives. We are both the broken cup and the hands that mend it. The gold that fills the cracks is made from the way we honor the break, the meaning we choose to make, the love we allow in, and the growth we lean into. When we make a repair, when we honor our own fractures instead of hiding them, we do not just return to

The Call to Live Real

what we were. We become something more. Something even more whole, multidimensional, and beautiful, not despite the breaks but *because* of them.

That's how Realing works, too. Every time we feel the sting of sadness, *Realing* can help us process it in a way that expands our capacity to both be in the moment and to open for joy, delight, and happiness on the other side. We all have this ability within us.

I wrote this book to help us find our way back to ourselves. To help us clarify what matters, be more present, be more resilient, and no longer let go of the precious moments life offers us. Adversity can be disorienting, yet it's also defining and has the potential to be transformative, to be a threshold moment of possibility.

I hope, in these pages, you find space to step away from the busyness of life and to find your way back to you.

There are three distinct parts to the Realing Journey:

Part I: The Problem of Shallowing

When we strip back everything and take an honest look at what has made us miss out on our lives—the numbness, the burnout, the curated versions of self we have been performing for too long—we can explore both the false beliefs we have lived under, and the quiet crisis of disconnection that's eroded our sense of aliveness. You will be able to see how we have traded depth for dopamine and connection for control. And perhaps most importantly, you will come to realize that it is not your fault. But it is your responsibility.

Part II: The Opportunity to Real

Understanding the problem creates the leverage and gateway to engage in all of life. As we explore the mindsets essential for stopping racing and starting to remember, you will meet the core practices of Realing. You will learn how to listen inward, reclaim your nervous system, emotional range, and presence. This is where feelings that were once numbed break open into knowing.

Part III: A Guide for Living Real

Realing is not a one-time revelation; it's a way of being. Integrating tools and practices, we build the mindset to live more Real. We will explore how to embrace the complex parts that inevitably arise as we build our capacity to live with more depth. By doing so, you awaken to your own true presence, one that's more vibrant, complex, and profoundly alive. This is beyond knowing what it means to be Real, but to live it.

If any of these statements apply to you, you are in the right place:

- You are successful by external metrics, but feel an empytiness rather than fulfillment.
- You move through your days feeling flat, numb, disconnected.
- You crave deeper, more genuine relationships, yet struggle to form genuine intimacy.
- You have so much, and yet sense something essential is missing.
- You find yourself caught in endless cycles of achievement and exhaustion.
- The thought of feeling deeply both compels and terrifies you.
- Something whispers to you that there must be more than this half-lived existence.

Realing is the conscious acceptance that life is messy, difficult experiences happen, and ignoring them does not make them disappear. Ignoring them may feel good in the moment, but it only pushes the uncomfortable feelings beneath the surface of our conscious mind. Left there, they shape us in unseen, but very palpable ways, impacting every area of our lives. It's only through honestly confronting the tension created by our most painful truths that we can disarm them.

Realing is a transformative journey that awaits you. A journey where you will learn to create connections that feel sincere and unforced. Where you'll find support that comes naturally to you. Where laughter will fill you genuinely. Where joy will show up in ways you've never even imagined. These shifts will transform your relationships and life into something infinitely richer and more rewarding.

You were never meant to live Shallow. You were meant to be present, live fully, and feel deeply. A more meaningful path is waiting. Will you take the first step?

Let's begin.

PART I

THE PROBLEM OF SHALLOWING

In this section, we'll explore this problem in depth, attempting to understand the curse of *Shallowing*, what it is, how we got here, and the actual costs it imposes on us, our loved ones, and our communities. Together, we'll examine the stories, assumptions, and values we have inherited and internalized, many of which no longer serve us.

The truth is, most of us are living unwell. To create meaningful change, we must first acknowledge what's at stake, recognize the prices we are paying—both individually and collectively—and identify the choices available to help us live more fully and authentically. This kind of truth-telling demands candor, courage, and compassion. Honesty is always the first step toward transformation.

Living Real is a deeply vulnerable act. It takes courage to be uncomfortable, to be deeply honest, and to question how we have been living. It's only when we understand this that we give ourselves a choice for something different.

If you already feel the weight of Shallowness and maybe even understand why you've lived that way, feel free to begin with Part II, so you can move directly into solutions. But for those who want the leverage that comes from truly understanding the cost of Shallowing, who are willing to sit with the truth long enough to let it shift something within, read on.

ONE

THE CURSE OF THE SHALLOWS

By avoiding hard things, we unknowingly, preemptively forfeit or diminish our joy.

As a business psychologist, I'm paid to be present, to ask hard questions, and to be Real. Throughout this book, I'll share client stories to illustrate concepts. Most names have been changed to preserve anonymity. While many stories are about leaders, their challenges apply to most of us.

When clients first engage me, many arrive with polished personas and professional aspirations. These individuals are already financially successful and eager to achieve *more* within their ever-expanding ambitions. They want to be better leaders, earn their next promotion, or manage their time more effectively. Many have adequately masked their self-doubt, disease, or loneliness, even to themselves.

As they settle in and share their stories, many often begin to shift simply because I am fully present. It can be "enough" to have someone be Real for you. One CEO, Peter, missed only one session in the fifty-two weeks we worked together. It often takes only a few sessions for most of them to realize how disconnected they are. They recognize how they've spent years hyper-focused on what's next, only to find they've watched their lives pass them by. I hear them speak of restlessness, discontent, and the feeling that something essential is missing or slipping away from them. I see the desperation in their eyes as they think, *How can my life look so perfect on paper and still feel so devoid of meaning?*

That question resonates with many people these days. We are busy working hard yet deeply curious, longing to listen inward to ourselves.

Life as a Sine Wave

Our lives are made up of a combination of our experiences, the oscillation of highs and lows. Imagine drawing a steady wave across a piece of paper, rising to a peak, dipping down into a valley, and repeating endlessly. In life, we have experiences that range in the same way. Life is like a sine wave—rising and falling with predictable unpredictability.

And that means WE are the sum of that wave, a combination of our life experiences. We are so much more than our accomplishments, bank accounts, and "success." We comprise relationships, connections, memories, moments in time, and encounters. The more we pay attention to the full spectrum of our experiences, the richer our lives can be.

Highs of Life

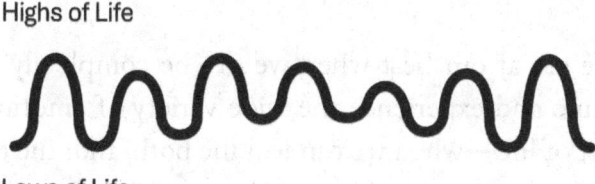

Lows of Life

When my grandmother died, it was my first actual encounter with the extreme low of loss. It was a grief intense enough to hollow me. I imagine we have all savored unforgettable memories, felt significant loss, and wondered what to do with heartache. It was my late father who helped me move through it by seeing the full range of the sine wave—how much my sorrow in losing her was a reflection of the heights of our love.

We all ride these waves of highs and lows. The question is not whether we will experience both happiness and sadness or grief and joy, but whether we will allow ourselves to fully feel both extremes. We've become conditioned to feel less and less of the lows, which results in our muting the experience of both.

> *[DEF] Sine Wave: The natural highs and lows of living. The arc of emotion, energy, and experience. Realing is about experiencing the full range of our individual Sine wave. It's not a problem to fix—it's the pulse of being human.*

We are at our best when we can be completely present over time and experience the wide variety of emotions that are part of life—when we can feel the both/and: the contrast between our ecstatic peaks and devastating valleys, between our celebrations and setbacks. Just as music is built from notes and silence, and pigment and space can define art, our lives find richness in these natural oppositions.

> **Ideas —> Action**
> Do you experience the full range of life?
> Where do you feel the highs and lows?
> Where does life feel more muted?

The Power of Full Presence

I woke up on September 14, 1995, to a brief, emotional phone call that changed my understanding of what a "good life" meant. Having just returned from working in Africa, I was about to start a doctoral program in psychology. I'd barely settled into my new apartment 600 miles from home when my father called to tell me that my grandmother had died.

My grandmother, whom I lovingly called Nanny, meant the world to me. During my childhood, I spent every summer living with her. As the youngest of my cousins, I often sought respite with her whenever I fell behind. She always felt available. Some of my favorite moments were snuggling on the loveseat on her screened-in porch or watching a storm approach across the lake.

As she patiently brushed the snarls from my rats' nest hair, she never commented that I hadn't showered for weeks, even though she knew. And she could always be counted on for a sweet. While the world knew her as a tart, sharp-tongued widow, to me, she was home, offering me compassion and an endless source of reverent, unconditional love.

Instead of immediately trying to comfort me, negate my sadness, or remind me that Nanny was old and unwell, my father simply gave me his full presence. He listened to my broken heart, and when I finally paused, he offered an insight that transformed my awareness.

"Sweetheart, I want you to feel it all. Feel how sad you are," he told me. "This is a huge loss, and your heart aches."

Confused, I sobbed a bit longer, wondering why he would want me to feel worse. A moment later, he explained, "I want you to celebrate that you and Nanny had an incredibly special connection—a love like few others. Feeling the depth of your sadness is the best tribute to the height of your love."

In that simple conversation, he gave new meaning to complicated feelings, while recognizing, even celebrating, the full range of my Real emotions.

My father helped me understand that sorrow is not merely a burden, but also an opportunity. Heartache is a tribute to our capacity for joy and delight. It's a sign of how deeply we have loved. His words helped me grasp the importance of living the full range of our emotions. That this moment with my father coincided with the beginning of my doctoral journey, added layers of meaning to my personal and professional evolution.

Realing is experiencing the full range of life.
Highs of Life

Lows of Life

Engaging the Full Range

As we ride the rise and fall of life's waves, the question becomes whether we will meet those highs and lows with presence. Whether we will allow ourselves to feel the full spectrum of grief and joy, sorrow and delight, without turning away. Whether we will allow ourselves to be present for both extremes. Because therein lies the heart of living.

In my grief, it became clear to me just how many people do not access the full spectrum of emotions in their lives. What began as a playful exploration became a passion. I started by looking at myself, then included my family, and then added in clients, until I finally saw it everywhere.

The more presence I brought to experiencing the full range of human emotions—at work, in life, with clients, globally—the more apparent it was who around me struggled with and in their feelings. What I saw was that our failure to be Real was not just lessening our existence, but also threatening our well-being, both individually and collectively, even globally.

We crave feeling vibrantly alive, and ideally loved. Too often, we associate being accepted with feeling loved. We hide away our metaphoric warts, the parts of ourselves where we feel shame or fear others' judgment. At the same time, we polish our rough edges and present the sides of ourselves that we think others "like," all in our desire to feel accepted or liked.

Shallowing is

Avoiding discomfort, hard experiences, or uncomfortable emotions.

We feel worse for being disingenuous. We don't want to work so hard, put on a show, or even try to explain why. The people with whom we engage feel worse, too. When we hide the essence of who we are or cover up our flaws, they see us and think: *Wow, she's so happy, why can't I be? How does she do it all and seem so perfect? What's wrong with me?*

In contrast, consider my dear friend Ryan who wanted to mark February 2, 2022—2/2/22—with a Tuba-Tutu parade. As in two-ba and two-two. In anticipation of the two-filled date, he made over 50 colorful tutus. He invited two friends who each played the tuba to join his shenanigans. At 10 am that morning, they met on Main Street of their hometown, a Utah ski village, to hand out tutus. Ryan then invited friends and strangers to participate in his Tuba-Tutu parade—they laughed, celebrated, and hugged for a mile. Through his authenticity and sharp wit, he created silly, clean fun that sparked joy in participants and observers alike.

We need more moments like this. Instead, our fractured society is overflowing with isolation, burnout, anxiety, and depression. It is a manifestation of the Shallowing of our lives and something that has been in the making for years. We crave opportunities to connect and join in magic, like Ryan's Tuba-Tutu parade, but have fallen into habits and behaviors that contribute to further fracturing.

Shallowing:
Truncates our ability to feel Joy, Happiness or Fulfillment

Because we avoid discomfort, hard experiences or uncomfortable emotions.

The House Metaphor

While the following metaphor applies to us collectively as a community, let's start on the individual level. Imagine your life as a two-story house with a basement. Whenever something hard, painful, embarrassing, or uncomfortable happens, you stuff it into that mental basement, hoping to forget it as quickly as possible.

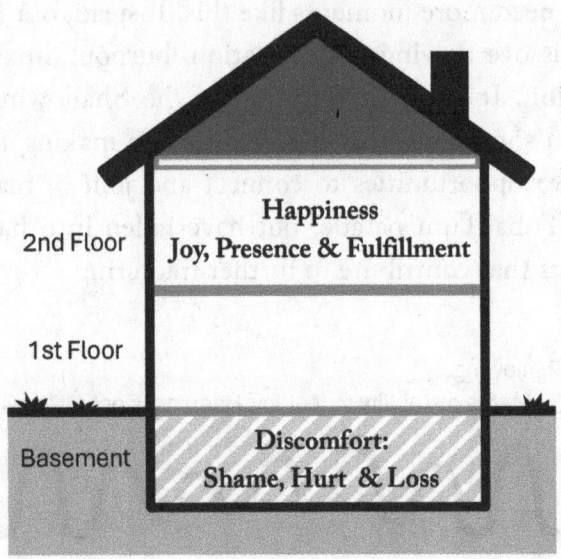

Somewhere along the way, you have learned—whether consciously or not—that instead of feeling the complex emotions, we can aim to avoid the discomfort altogether. That may feel better in the short term, but stuffing away our feelings comes with risk. Psychotherapist Carl Jung said, "Until you make the unconscious conscious, it will direct your life, and you will call it fate."

> *[DEF] Basement: The space that holds "bad" or "hard" emotions. Feelings that are uncomfortable or that we don't like. Experiences we don't know how to feel or process. Examples include: Grief with*

no words. Rage with no outlet. Sadness that feels bottomless. Fear that contracts us.

At first, this practice of piling up painful emotions is no different from how we may clutter our physical basements with belongings that no longer serve us. For a while, it seems to work. Living this way will likely feel clean, easy, and simple because unpleasant emotions can be tucked away, out of sight, both to ourselves and others. This sort of emotional "refuse" disposal enables us to focus on the illusion of success or contentment without dealing with the distraction of any negative factors dragging us down.

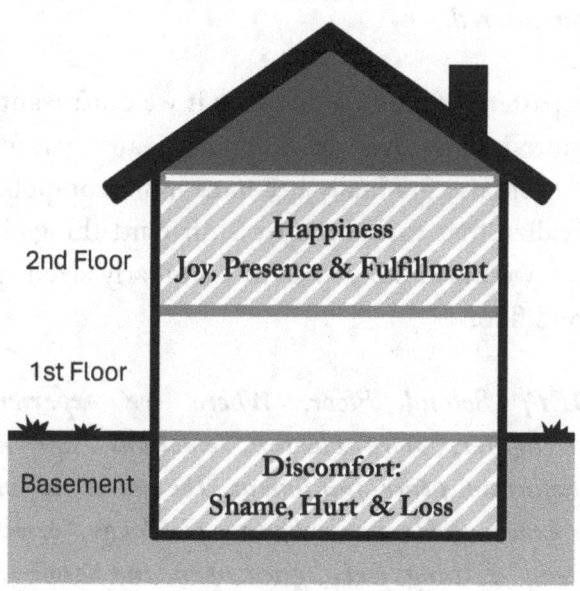

Over time, we believe that the visible part of our life is our whole life. Life is good, easy, and pretty on the first floor of our metaphoric house. We like that our Instagram lives look just like the Joneses, maybe even better. How we represent our life to the world is consistently optimized as fun and happy. But what we bury doesn't disappear; it becomes shadow. And the basement never forgets.

> *[DEF] First Floor: The face we present to the world. Where we live day-to-day—the part of us that we show others. It's our habits, expressions, and ways of showing up, which are not necessarily fake, but often filtered.*

This pattern of stuffing away what we don't want to face grows more intense over time. What began as an innocent, sporadic response gradually becomes more compulsive. We fail to realize that each time we stuff hard things into the basement, we block our access to a similarly sized space on the second floor.

> *[DEF] Second Floor: Where we experience our lighter, more pleasant emotions, like joy, satisfaction, peace, fulfillment. The spaces we wish we experienced more, when we feel "okay," or even "great," as things feel aligned, open, and flowing.*

We do not appreciate or anticipate that by refusing to face uncomfortable emotions, we also negate the positive ones. In the context of this house-of-self analogy, it's easy to see how this might create a more limited space for self-expression. Relationships become less emotional. Interactions become less genuine. Promotions and career success feel less satisfying. Life becomes less fulfilling as we grow Shallower.

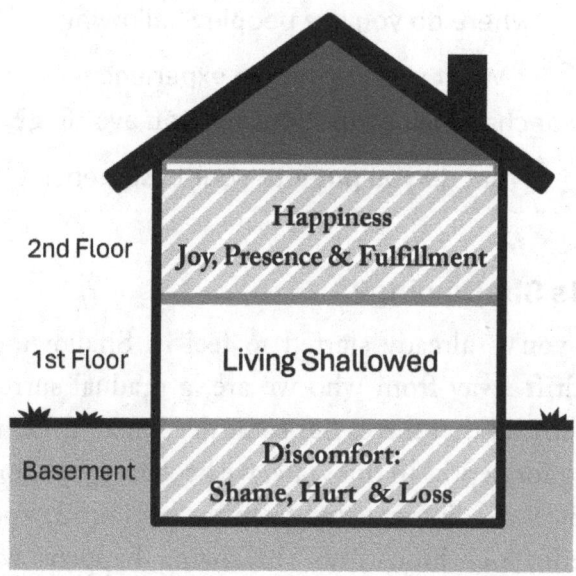

What was once a spacious home for our true selves becomes a cramped place, reflecting our Shallow existence. Eventually, we stuff away so many complex emotions in the basement that the house becomes unusable. Over time, the energy it takes to keep that stuff out of sight becomes exhausting. We're stuck with a basement full of rejected thoughts and emotions and a second floor full of equally inaccessible feelings of delight, happiness, and goodness.

> **Ideas —> Action**
>
> Reflecting on the house metaphor, where do you see people Shallowing?
>
> What uncomfortable experiences or challenging emotions are you avoiding?
>
> What do you put into your basement?

What Is Shallowing?

Maybe you've already started to feel it. Shallowing is the subtle drift away from who we are, a gradual surrender to the superficial that leaves our souls deadened, detached, and yearning for depth. In this state, we become spectators of our own existence, disconnected from the profound experiences that define our humanity. Shallowing happens when we skim the surface of life—when our attention fractures, our depth erodes.

Shallowing is often the unintended or unconscious result of avoiding difficult events and feelings. It happens when we cannot feel, engage, or be present with what is difficult. It's the narrowing of our lived, felt experience of life.

> *[DEF] Shallowing: The subtle, unconscious ways we mute feelings, narrow our existence, and limit emotions. How we avoid hard feelings and, in turn, unknowingly restrict our ability to feel joy, happiness, and fulfillment.*

We Shallow because it feels easier in the short term. Stabilizing. Most people do not understand the long-term consequences of Shallowing, and how it leads to disconnection, disengagement, and unwellness.

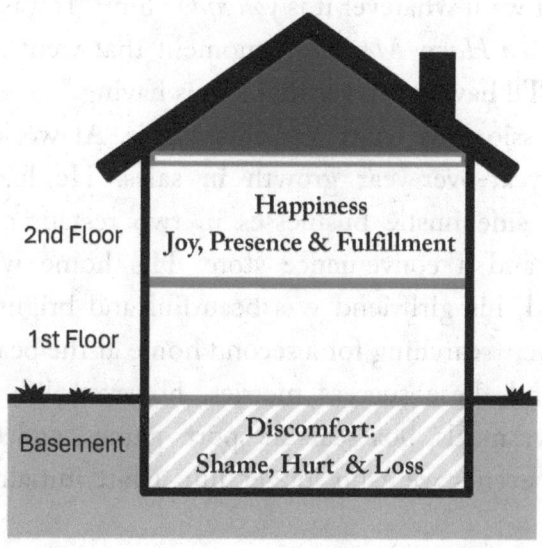

Shallowing:
Truncates our ability to feel Joy, Happiness or Fulfillment

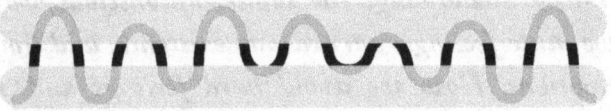

Because we avoid discomfort, hard experiences or uncomfortable emotions.

Recall the CEO client, Peter, who missed only one coaching conversation in our year-long collaboration. After witnessing Peter's transformation, a colleague hired me, saying: "I want whatever it is *you did to* him." It was an alpha male, *When Harry Met Sally*, moment that went along the lines of "I'll have whatever that guy is having."

Professionally, Matt was crushing it. At work, he was driving year-over-year growth in sales. He had several lucrative side hustle businesses in two restaurants, a dry cleaner, and a convenience store. His home was newly renovated, his girlfriend was beautiful and bright, and he was actively searching for a second home at the beach.

Behind these success metrics, however, life was flat. Expensive meals, box seats at sports games, and tickets to top-line events were no longer fun. Matt initially strayed from his relationship, wanting to feel more alive. Now, he only felt that zing when he bragged about the other women he had "bagged" to his direct reports. He kept looking to outside stimuli, craving the vitality he saw in his friend.

Refusing to feel lows truncates our ability to feel highs.

Shallowing appears easier in the short term; Long term, it stifles well-being.

Matt wanted to feel the full range of emotions—the vitality and happiness that is a part of living Real. He wanted to feel fully, but he was easily overcome and settled for the more external, ego-driven desire for more, better, faster. Like many of us, he had all the "wins," but he was looking outside of himself for his next high.

When his girlfriend moved out, saying, "You have everything you want, but I don't," a lightbulb went off. He was stumped by his lingering uncertainty, asking himself, *"What is it that I really want?"*

I understand the impulse to Shallow. We Shallow to avoid pain. Trying to avoid the lows of our lives feels almost instinctual, like running from something that's trying to hurt us. It can feel natural to want to avoid discomfort, numb our hurt, and keep emotions light, upbeat, and seemingly safe. But in doing so, we also forfeit the ability to feel the highs of our lives, because you can't selectively feel. You can't mute sadness without also dulling joy. You can't run from struggle and still expect to experience deep, soul-filling happiness.

This gradual surrender to the superficial leaves our souls yearning for depth. We become disconnected from the profound experiences that define our humanity. We overly attach to technology, other people's shoulds, and external distractions.

The Cost of Shallowing

Shallowing is contraction. It's pushing away what matters most, confining our most profound truths to that metaphorical basement of our consciousness. This creates emotional stagnation—a lack of flow that manifests as disease in both mind and body.

When stagnation takes hold, we lose flexibility, agility, and adaptability. More critically, we forfeit opportunities to gain clarity about what truly matters and mute our ability to feel supreme happiness, joy, or fulfillment. Although Peter and his buddy Matt were "crushing it," their world and lives had stagnated. Hanging out with the same types of people, doing the same kinds of things, and having the same type of conversations, they grew less and less alive as their world narrowed. They felt flat, but they didn't understand why. Coaching challenged their thinking, assumptions, and habits; our conversations offered a fresh perspective and opportunity.

We fail to acknowledge that when we bury the grief, fear, or heartbreak, we also bury our access to joy. By avoiding the shadows, we dim the light. By shielding ourselves from pain, we dull our capacity for wonder, connection, and love. Shallowing, in the short term, means grieving less deeply by lessening the intensity of our feelings. Longer-term, however, it stifles well-being. We think detachment protects us. But in truth, it erodes us. A numbness creeps in.

We hunger for vitality, for Real connection—but find ourselves unable to reach it. Our muted joy and sorrow leave us living in a narrow band of experience that barely resembles living at all. Ignoring, dismissing, or minimizing the hard stuff does not make it disappear—it just costs us access to what makes life meaningful. Just like our thinking gets contracted, our bodies also respond to stagnation, making it even more essential to engage in practices that restore flow: exercise, hydration, meditation, and other nurturing habits I will delve into in Part III.

Living Numb

Life can feel overwhelming at times for each of us. And we all have ways that we literally or metaphorically remove ourselves from stimuli, disengage from life, or detach emotionally. This is called numbing, and it is a way that we Shallow.

Done intentionally or in moderation, numbing can be adaptive and even healthy to navigate adversity. Remember Nancy Reagan and her bathing tip, "Calgon, take me away!" A bubble bath can be rejuvenating and do wonders for the psyche. Rather than numbing, it creates stillness, reflection, and renewal.

Unfortunately, too often, numbing and Shallowing have become the norm. Anything done in excess can become problematic, whether it's exercise, cleaning, drinking, eating, working, smoking, or porn. The first step is building awareness about our numbing patterns and what triggers these behaviors.

The challenge is that we live in a time that is far more overwhelming than ever before, and there are more and more easy ways to numb ourselves. Doom-scrolling. Watching cable news 24/7. Online shopping from Amazon at 3:00 a.m. Do any of these sound familiar?

Our digital habits amplify our ability to detach and numb. The numbers are staggering but unsurprising. According to a survey by Asurion, we check our smartphones ninety-six times daily and spend nearly seven hours a day staring at screens. Scrolling is a way we numb which leads to the Shallowing of our lives.

We are living over-wired. The paradox of technology is that constant digital connectivity creates the illusion of feeling more connected while disconnecting or disintermediating us from our surroundings. Technology has both imprisoned us and become our escape. We feel tethered to our devices, desperate to check in, and yet resentful that these devices limit our ability to be present, experience what's happening around us, and form genuine interpersonal connections.

> *[DEF] Numbing: The ways we disconnect from emotions that feel too much. How we learned to mute vulnerability, avoid uncertainty, or escape discomfort. Often unconscious, it can reduce or shield us from pain... but also from presence.*

Life can't and shouldn't be about chasing distraction. The shift into true numbness happens so gradually, you might barely notice it. The constant flicker between screens, the dopamine-laced rush of the next shiny object, the pressure to respond faster, do more, know everything—these distractions pull us out of presence. They can catapult us out of self, out of truth, and into numbness. This can manifest as feeling frozen or lacking the motivation to do what once brought you joy. Relationships that should nourish you can feel flat, almost transactional. It may seem like a compelling place to be, but the long-term cost is significant.

> ***Ideas —> Action***
>
> Where are you numbing in your life?
>
> What triggers you to numb out?

Navigating my way through a pretentious Beacon Hill cocktail party, I found myself alternating between dry crumpets and dry, superficial conversations. As I looked for the time, I debated filling my empty wine glass and the thought of more empty conversations. What was intended as a celebration was feeling more like penance. I remember my delight in seeing a friendly, Real face.

We dove deep into conversation, delighting in the impromptu, genuine catch-up. Moments later, an impeccably dressed, tart elder glared at us as we laughed. *Was she disapproving or jealous of the heartfelt connection?* She made her way through the crowded gathering and reprimanded us: "Has no one ever told you just how inappropriate it is to be discussing THAT, *here?*" Had I been sharper-witted and more courageous in the moment, I would have welcomed her into our Real exchange.

Beyond social gatherings, Shallowing can manifest as career milestones that once brought you satisfaction, but now feel routine, expected, or unfulfilling. When we numb, achievements that may have once defined our professional identity provide diminishing returns of fulfillment.

Countless times, clients bring their accomplishments to our conversations. We explore their recent success, whether it is a promotion, a successful deal closing, or conquering a new challenge. We delve into the stories and the feelings that are associated with them.

I often ask, "How are you celebrating?" I cringe, anticipating the response: "I'm celebrating right now with you." Sometimes, their relationships have thinned, and no one else really cares. Sometimes, they want to feel enlivened by their accomplishment but don't know how to create that within themselves, so they turn to me. Overly focused on work and emotionally Shallowed, there are few places they know where to turn for genuine interactions.

In this numbing thinness, we begin to mistake volume for value, reaction for reflection, and noise for knowing. And slowly, almost imperceptibly, we lose our capacity for depth, for the inner stillness where Real understanding forms and insight roots. We become scattered in mind and spirit. We become Shallowed.

We internalize the belief that this limited, surface-level existence is just how life is. We assume Real depth, genuine feeling, is not possible—or worse, is not worth it. But it is. And reclaiming our lives changes *everything*.

Many of us have unconsciously bought into illusions we have seen projected out into the world. We've bought into the expectations and assumptions we were raised to believe about life, such as:

- Happiness is ...
- A good life is ...
- Hard things happen, but the faster you move on from them, the better. ("Can't you move on already? Look at her, she has it so much worse.")

We've bought into the idea that difficult things will cease to exist if we eliminate, delete, or gloss over them. We've deluded ourselves into thinking we're doing all of this "to be nice," believing we're being kind to avoid burdening others with negativity, and assuming that those around us wouldn't want to know.

We have failed to appreciate that even when we don't adequately acknowledge the hard and hurtful things that happen, they don't go away. So, when we minimize feeling bad about the negatives or focus only on the positives, even in the short term, we set up patterns with dire long-term consequences.

As a Rhodes scholar, Joe was often celebrated for his brilliance. He transitioned with agility between several careers, including writing, finance, and ultimately became a strategic consultant. He rose quickly to the top of each field. Behind his intellect was a capacity to feel deeply, fully, and sometimes in ways that felt "too much." Alcohol became an easy gateway to numb feelings of discomfort. It helped the pain fade or mute it entirely, even if only briefly. He felt more social and could release intense emotions, and for a long time, no one seemed to notice.

When we scroll instead of speaking, nod instead of listening, or feel numb instead of feeling—sometimes not even Realizing we're doing it—it's clear something's missing. Life feels ... off. Not broken, necessarily, but dulled. Like a song we can no longer hear, though we remember it used to move us.

We feel frustrated that we've been doing all the right things and feel as though none of it is making a difference. This is because so much of what we are doing is not Real. It's not rooted or alive with purpose or power. We've learned how to function but not how to feel. We've mastered coping but not connection. And when connections fade, meaning thins. There's a reason we feel like something isn't right. There's a reason we are tired in ways sleep can't fix. It's because we are living *around* our lives, not *in* them.

A Return to Real

With my father's help, I learned both the sacredness of grieving and how not to be Shallow. My father didn't force light into dark moments. He didn't sidestep emotion or smooth the sharp edges of grief. He stayed present quietly, wholly, and without flinching. In doing so, he permitted me to feel. To fall apart. To be human.

This was Realing, though I didn't recognize it back then. Rather than allowing me to suppress the full anguish of my sorrow in a reflexive effort to comfort myself, my father was present for me in a way that allowed me to be Real. He helped me face and *feel* my emotional pain instead. In doing so, he also helped me expand my heart's capacity to feel *everything*. It is only now, years later, that I have realized what a true gift my father's presence was, as he, too, was grieving himself.

Living Real is enjoying your whole house, the happiness and the discomfort.

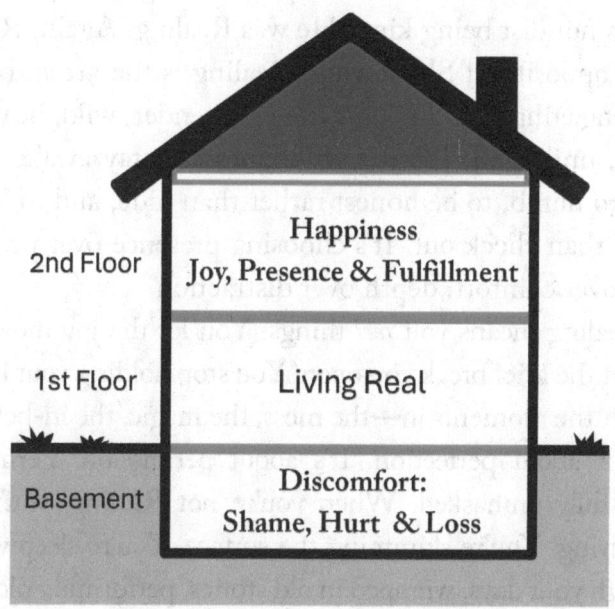

Living Real is experiencing the full range of experiences and emotions.

Until recently, I didn't have language for what I had experienced with my father—and in contrast what I had longed for in other relationships. Looking back, I see now he was not just being kind. He was Realing. Again, Realing is the opposite of Shallowing. Realing is the art and act of fully engaging with life *as it is*—raw, tender, wild, beautiful, brutal, unfiltered. It's the willingness to stay awake rather than go numb, to be honest rather than hide, and to lean in rather than check out. It's choosing presence over pretense, truth over comfort, depth over distraction.

Realing means you *feel* things. You let the joy move you. You let the grief break you open. You stop holding your breath. You let the moments in—the mess, the magic, the in-between. It's not about perfection. It's about permission. Permission to be fully unmasked. When you're not Realing, you're not fully living. You're skimming the surface. You're sleepwalking through your days, wrapped in old stories, performing old roles, reacting from old wounds. You might be busy, productive, or even seem "fine"—but you're not home. You're not fully in your body, life, or the truth of what's here and now.

Realing brings you back:

Back to your senses.

Back to your knowing.

Back to what matters.

Back to yourself.

It's not always easy. It rarely is. Because Realing requires courage, it asks you to feel what you've been avoiding, confront what's been concealed, and stand in the fire of your awakening. But that fire is also what forges your freedom.

Realing does not make life prettier—it makes it truer. And in that truth, a deeper kind of beauty emerges. One that does not need fixing or faking. One that cracks you open and fills you with light. So, when I say *'Real,'* I don't mean just being honest. I mean alive. Present. Unhidden. I mean you, choosing to inhabit your own life from the inside out. Let that be the invitation of Realing moving forward.

Why Realing? Why Now?

We live in a world padded with illusion—curated lives, constant performance, and a chase for self-worth that never feels enough. But underneath it, something in us is stirring. We are waking up. We are aching for something Real again.

When people stop to get perspective, when the noise of daily demands fades, a clear view of what matters most remains. Whether this is a still point or near the end of one's life, people are not haunted by the things they did not earn, they are haunted by the ways they did not live. They do not speak of money or titles. They speak of time lost. Of love withheld. Of laughter missed. And loved ones, if they are there, often stand by with heavy hearts, wondering why it took so long to see what mattered most.

What surfaces again and again for many people are the choices they *didn't* make—the times they played small, muted themselves, or chased someone else's version of success. Some reflect on how they traded their authenticity for acceptance, their presence for productivity, and their peace for perfection. They remember what they *didn't* say. The people they drifted from. The joy they postponed. They begin to see how often they deferred their aliveness, hoping someday would come—and how rarely it did.

These aren't regrets in the traditional sense. They recognize that they have lived at arm's length from what is most Real. They acknowledge bypassing the simple, sacred things—honesty, connection, freedom, joy—in pursuit of safety or belonging. The cost was not visible at the time. But now, with everything stripped away, it's obvious.

What is most painful is not just Realizing the truth, but also accepting it. It's Realizing there's no more time left to live it. We do not have to wait until the end or a wake-up call to start truly living.

Two

THE LIES WE WERE SOLD

*Will you wake up to what matters before
it is too late?*

All too often, we continue with the traditions, beliefs, and patterns of our youth. Many of us accepted certain norms and expectations at face value. We believed what we were told, absorbed the messages in our environment, and then went on autopilot with family beliefs, cultural norms, and definitions of success.

I recall my college professor describing how she intentionally chose her religion before starting a family. She explored six different faith traditions, studying their beliefs and practices before choosing Judaism. Raised an Episcopalian, I had accepted that as my inherited religion without thinking or contrasting it. Yet, if faith is something that guides our actions and becomes our moral compass, shouldn't it be chosen intentionally? Until then, it had never occurred to me that there were choices at my disposal or that, as an adult, I could be entirely in the driver's seat of my own life.

If you are reading this book, you, like that professor, are ready and hoping to be more intentional in your choices and to step into the entirety of who you are. Culturally, we are in a period of amplification. Ideas, emotions, and behaviors are being magnified, intensified, or spread more rapidly, regardless of whether they are good or bad. For many of us, it has become clear that what we have been doing is no longer working in various Realms of our lives, whether individually, collectively, or both. There is an invitation—an urgency, in fact—to question assumptions, feel more fully, and be more Real.

Embracing the Unexpected

Dave reached out to me after reading an article I had written in *Psychology Today*. Anticipating an internal job search for a CEO role, he wanted to be the leading candidate for that promotion. Witty and self-aware, Dave knew he would need a little fine-tuning to be his company's top choice. He had received feedback that he was ready to tackle, so he hired me.

Three weeks into our collaboration, he shared a story from a recent long weekend he had spent with his family. He offhandedly mentioned that he'd stumbled while walking up the stone stairs from the lake to the house. I listened to his story with a sense that something was off. The stumbling didn't feel accidental, so I gently nudged him to consider a visit to his physician.

What came next was a blur of appointments that resulted in him being diagnosed with Parkinson's disease. Dave quickly pivoted away from seeking the coveted CEO role and dove deep into a personal journey of managing his future by understanding the costs, implications, and medical ramifications of this diagnosis. *What did he need to know? How did he need to change his life? What did this diagnosis mean for him, his family, and his future?*

To walk beside someone as their life trajectory is transformed is humbling. I witnessed Dave's aspirations shift, his dream of becoming CEO dissipate, and his idea of what it truly meant to live a good life completely transform. I was with him as he became fully present in his health and saw, with crisp focus, what mattered now and the lies he had bought into that had steered him astray.

Have you gone through a moment like this? Or have you witnessed something like this in a friend? Bad news can be profoundly clarifying. Dave rapidly honed in on all the different ways his life would change. Fitness became the golden ticket to preserving his quality of life, a gift he could no longer take for granted, because time was not on his side.

Suddenly, his Peleton was transformed from a clothing horse into a machine for strength, vitality, and hope. Years earlier, he had started journals for each of his kids but never found the time to work on them. What had felt like a "should do" was a time-sensitive "want to do." Dave quickly realized that fulfillment and true happiness come from genuine connections, being of service, and living *a life of* service.

Many have asked, "How did you know from that story that his stumble was problematic?"

We often listen to the words to gain cognitive understanding. When we are fully tuned in, there is wisdom or knowing that comes with a full-bodied presence. I had practiced this for years, such that when I was listening to Dave's story, I felt a vibration in my lower abdomen that was distinctly different. This is the true power of presence and Realing. We will delve deeper into this in Part III, but first, we need to understand the beliefs, myths, and lies that inhibit us and create regret.

The Lies We Believe

This chapter is not intended to point blame. It's meant to illuminate how our assumptions, norms, and beliefs can lead us to distort truth, often in an attempt to avoid discomfort or vulnerability. It's intended to interrupt false Realities—the illusions that we have inherited, absorbed, or created, perhaps under pressure and likely without knowing.

I hope you will question some of the stories and beliefs that we live by, discard what feels oppressive or incongruous, and hold on to what feels empowering. But you can only do that once you acknowledge the distorted beliefs in your life and recognize how our culture, families, and numerous other factors have reinforced what may not be serving you.

Here are some to consider:

Myth #1 Success is Money, Power, and Fame

Over the past twenty years, as a business psychologist, I have spent time with some of the most accomplished people in the world: leaders, visionaries, and high performers. I've seen actions and heard fears firsthand that most had never spoken aloud. Many of these people have been quietly, sometimes desperately, suffering. Behind the accolades and wealth, they were starving for something more. Often, not more success, but more *life*. More joy. More aliveness.

We know their names. We've read the headlines. Tony Hsieh, founder of Zappos, was one of them. With two successful exits, he was celebrated and revered. And still, that wasn't enough to keep him alive. He died in a suspicious fire that may have been linked to his drug use. He, like far too many others, seemed to have it all. His death at age 46 points toward a very different reality.

The statistics about stimulants—drugs, alcohol, sex—reveal a desperate search from so many to feel something. And still, the myth persists that success equals happiness. That money secures meaning. If we can climb high enough, fast enough, far enough, then we'll finally feel okay. But look closer, and you will see the cracks. The numbing. The coping. The stimulants and addictions that patch over a deeper ache.

Many of us were conditioned to believe that feelings are a distraction, that introspection is indulgent, and that success belongs only to those who work harder, push through, and ignore the voice inside telling them something is off. We were sold a lie.

We may have learned to measure our worth in tangible items we could count—titles, paychecks, followers—while neglecting intangibles like our authenticity, relationships, and a sense of purpose. So, why are so many who "make it" still lost or unfulfilled? Why do they chase more only to feel less? Because the lie was never designed to make us happy. It was designed to keep us chasing.

We do not want more *stuff*. We want to *feel*. To be lit up. To come alive within this world that keeps asking us to perform instead of belong. So, we continue to chase uppers and peak experiences, convinced they'll solve our emptiness. But they never do for very long.

Myth #2 Perfection Is Possible

As social media continues to grow, almost everyone has some form of online presence. Many of us navigate the tightrope between: *Who am I? Who does the world think I am? And who do I want the world to think I am?* It can be hard to genuinely integrate our inner identities with the outer image. We've all created a carefully curated version of ourselves. Typically, this is one that depicts a sunny, successful, well put together façade, all the while hiding the "uglies" in our metaphorical basement.

> *[DEF] Instagram Life: The external identity we project, regardless of whether or not we are on social media. The carefully curated image we share rather than the truth we live. The highlight reel we show others is polished, pretty, and often performative. It is solely the good, skips the messy parts, and hides what's Real.*

We've been fed the lie and believe that perfection is possible. Again, whether you're on social media or not, many of us still try to maintain the illusion of an Instagram life in our everyday lives. We put on makeup to go grocery shopping. We pretend that life is "fine" after we lose our jobs. We return to work quickly after a loved one dies.

We feel pressure to be just as involved as stay-at-home moms, baking all the sourdough bread, making cute lunches, and having outfits for every season. Now, we share carefully curated, messy moments to appear more authentic. We post fake struggles the way you might share "weaknesses" in a job interview.

When did we forget that messy happens? It's okay to have dirty dishes in the sink as we take a nap instead of sipping that third cup of coffee to power through the day. It's okay to stay at home when you don't have the budget for a vacation.

Even though our Instagram life only represents a fraction of who we truly are, it can feel easier to hide behind a mask in our interactions, such as wearing a smile through a difficult meeting or sending out happy holiday cards during a divorce. After all, we have been taught that it's important to maintain appearances at all costs.

Through this meticulous personal branding, most of us project the image of who we aspire to be, who the world told us we should be, or who we hope the world will believe we are. And all the while, we hide the unattractive aspects of ourselves deep in our psyche, keeping the basement door of that place firmly shut. We don't want anyone to see our angst, worry, or self-doubt.

So, how is it we move away from this sort of being? In 2023, many full-time content creators stepped away from their online personas. Some disappeared without even saying goodbye. We started noticing as they came back, rested and full of life again. They began to take a stand against the always-on, always-producing cycle they were living in. They let go of the perfected version of themselves. Their platforms were forever changed by their willingness to be Real. So, this leads me to ask you this: If they can do this, why can't we? Are you ready for the shift back into wholeness?

Myth #3 Achieving Is Winning, And More Is Better

Most people come to me chasing some version of success they've been taught to want. They want more achievement, more influence, more wealth. On paper, it appears to be progress. In their minds, it will bring happiness. A fulfilling life. A good life.

We are encouraged and positively reinforced for pursuing what we want intensively. The more we delude ourselves that success (and thus happiness) come from accomplishments, the more apt we are to relentlessly push forward.

John built his career with laser-like precision. A Division I athlete in college, after graduation, work became his new sport and identity. Wired for competition, he dove in, determined to conquer. Winning deals brought a warm feeling that quickly became addictive. The more success he achieved, the more fiercely he focused on deals and capriciously he took risks.

John did most of the "right" things. Marrying Stacy felt like the logical next step, as did buying a house close to the highly reviewed preschool. Intensely focused on more, better, and faster, he celebrated promotions with a gift for his wife and a photo to share. Competing became so captivating that he no longer recognized why he wanted to win or what felt good.

Sound familiar? Beneath the striving and proving, John wanted the validation and connection he had felt on the soccer field. When you sit at the end of your life, will you think back to the accolades or the moments and memories you missed obtaining them? We can have both, but it takes someone who is fully aware of the boundaries necessary to do so.

Chasing the illusion that "winning at work" is "winning in life" is yet another way we Shallow. High achievers wear masks of success so convincingly that they forget they are wearing them.

I guarantee you can always find someone who is living bigger and better than you. At the root of it, we all want to feel we are enough. This isn't something we can do or think our way into. It has to be felt, lived, and embodied. It has to settle into the bones and spaces where doubt lives.

True "enough-ness" is not something we earn—it's something we feel, know, and own. It comes when we live Real.

Myth #4 Something Can Make You Enough

It's one of our deepest desires to be loved fully as we are. And yet, we live in this always-on, always judging, always comparing world. We're deeply connected to other people's successes and our own shortcomings.

Many people lament, often with quiet frustration, about Impostor Syndrome, that persistent inner murmur that whispers: *You're not qualified, you're just faking it, any moment now, they'll find out you're not the Real deal.* It's the sense that you are pretending to be someone or something you're not. Whether that's true or not, simply having that feeling shapes how you experience and interact with the world.

[DEF] Impostor Syndrome: Feelings of self-doubt, incompetence, lack of achievement, combined with a fear of others' perceiving you as a fraud (despite evidence of accomplishments and competence). A sense that I do not belong or deserve to be here.

In many ways, feeling like an impostor is a symptom of Shallowness. It arises when we start measuring our messy, beautiful humanity against the curated surfaces of others. We forget everyone else has bloopers, too. We compare our insides to their highlight reels.

We retreat with our voice, creativity, and connection. We self-diminish. And it can feel like the ground beneath us is thinning. Slowly, we stop trying to be more like ourselves and start trying to be more like them. It's in that narrowing that we lose contact with our own richness. Not because we are not enough, but because we have stepped out of alignment with our own wholeness.

Rather than judging yourself for this impostor feeling, instead of thinking it means something is wrong, and stuffing it into the metaphoric basement, try looking at it as a signpost. Impostor Syndrome can be a benefit if you see it as a signal that you are longing for greater mastery, deeper alignment, and a sense of wholeness.

Myth #5 There is More Time

Time has a way of passing us by almost imperceptibly. (Unless you are holding plank position! Nothing slows down time more than plank). Time is an illusion. It's not that we need to live in fear of our time. Instead, we need to spend it in ways that bring us to life—pulses through our bodies, bends us in grief, opens us in awe, and collapses us in stillness.

My father liked to joke, "When you're young, you're broke; when you're old, you're bent." Too often, we spend our youth chasing money, only to later spend our money chasing our youth—all the while, missing out on just how valuable our time is.

We may measure our worth by how much we can do inside a billable hour, but we were never meant to live like machines. There are moments that seem to last forever: a glance, a last breath, a somber goodbye. And there are years that vanish into nothing because we were never entirely in them.

Maybe this is the Real wound. Not that time is running out, but that we have been running past our lives, missing out on what only happens when we slow down enough to feel. At the breakneck pace some of us are moving, we're losing opportunities left and right. Losing the chance to take risks. Wrongly assuming we have enough time left—until we don't.

When urgency drives us, we default to safety. We repeat instead of reinventing anew, settle instead of stretching. We choose the known pain over the unknown freedom because, at least, it fits into the calendar. Risk does not always look like burning it all down. Sometimes it's soft and subtle.

- Like resting when the world tells you to hustle
- Like speaking even when your voice shakes
- Like trusting that your timing is your own, and you do not have to match anyone else's pace

The risk is not in moving too slowly. The risk is in never allowing yourself to move differently. The belief that there will always be more time, another opportunity, robs us of being in the here and now.

Myth # 6 Busy Is Better

We've bought into the ideology that busy people are somehow more important and that long hours are a badge of virtuous dedication. "I'm so busy," we say, with that strange mixture of complaint and pride, implying that our exhaustion is a badge of honor.

I see it every day: clients who are overwhelmed, overextended, exhausted, and burned out. They can recount all that their peers are doing. They lament that they have less and less time for the things that matter. They know they are less healthy, less present with their loved ones, and less fulfilled, and yet they still raise their hand for more work.

These beliefs fan our fear: *If I'm not busy, I must not be doing it right. I must not be important. I must not be enough.* There's a latent anxiety: *If I disconnect too long, someone will replace me.* People feel guilty for resting, even for spending time with family. They believe they must always be available to save the day, the moment the subsequent fire ignites.

We've started defining busy as being better. Because we operate on overload as a default, it becomes all we know. We believe the illusion that success favors those who hustle harder and push faster—and that becomes our permission to avoid the deeper, harder internal work of Realing.

Being too busy becomes the excuse for why your Shallowed marriage fell apart, why you failed to have that critical conversation, or how you overlooked a significant health problem. The aching feelings were inside of you, but you didn't stop long enough to listen inward. You might not have even known how to listen inward.

It's easy to fill space. It's much harder to sit in the discomfort that stillness creates. A full calendar doesn't equal a whole life. There's a hidden belief that if we keep moving, we will outrun the ache we do not want to feel. But living Shallowed always catches up with us, one way or another.

Myth #7 Being Still Is Falling Behind

Many of us stay busy out of fear that if we pause and enjoy the moment, we will fall behind. As we always overfill our schedules with never-ending to-do lists, many of us have lost our ability to be still. We routinely overlook our current achievements, focusing only on what's to come.

Lack of stillness is another way we Shallow ourselves, protecting ourselves from feeling a range of emotions. Rather than listening inward and taking a few hours to sleep or a weekend without notifications, we reach for our phones. Disconnected from our bodies and feelings, we no longer know what we need.

Behind our busyness is a nagging fear:

- If I don't do this now, it will only get worse.
- If I stop, even for a moment, I'll lose momentum.
- If I don't keep checking, I'll miss something important.

- If I don't stay busy, I'll fall short of expectations, of opportunity, of what others expect of me or what I expect of myself.
- If I don't stay on the treadmill, I'll fall off altogether.

But what if this weight is not in the task itself? What if this heaviness comes from the story we've told ourselves, the one we've believed, about what will happen if we don't do "blank" right now?

There is a hidden truth that so many of us carry—barely audible but always present: If I take a breath, if I step off the gas, I'll fall behind. In reality, when we force ourselves to do more, we often end up having to backtrack later. Because when we pause, we gain perspective and become present to what we actually need. We can fully process, understand, and integrate feelings, metabolizing the emotions and moving beyond them rather than suppressing or avoiding them.

So, the Real question is not: *How far behind will I fall if I pause?* The Real question is this: *What am I missing when I don't wait?*

Many of my clients fear stillness. They equate being still with being idle, lazy, or obsolete, consumed by a pervasive, latent fear of falling behind. I am reminded of Steve, a managing director of a global consulting firm. After years of service, he was eligible for a six-month paid sabbatical.

He had seven years to use it before losing it. Weeks before his sabbatical was due to expire, and the clock would reset to zero time accrued, Steve begrudgingly went on leave.

Initially, he struggled to unplug from the teams he mentored, the business he had been developing, and the projects he had shepherded. But at some point, during the nine weeks, Steve started to realize just how activated he had been by the adrenaline, cortisol, stress, and intensity of his travel, demands, and long hours.

In stepping away, Steve regained his health, began to grieve his mother's death (which had occurred four years earlier), delved back into house projects, and was reminded of how much he enjoyed incubating and creating. Toward the end, even Steve and his wife feared that he might not return to the intense, albeit lucrative, work. Time away drastically changed his life and markers of success.

Beyond the misguided belief that taking a breath is tantamount to catastrophe, there's a more profound fear for many of us: a hidden fear. That if we get perspective and calibrate on what really matters, we might never find the momentum to restart. We might see what we crave and be drawn towards that change. *Then what would we do?*

If we are brave enough to give stillness a chance, we can discover that stillness brings the potential for a new way forward.

When we pause, we

- Get perspective;
- Become more present to what we need; and
- Metabolize hard emotions, and see how they transform.

Myth #8 We Can Explain Everything, with Certainty and Knowing

We've been told that if we work harder, learn more, do enough, and keep achieving, we can be in control. We believe in certainty, just as we clung to the false beliefs about success, perfection, and winning, in the hopes of simply "being enough." Research shows that achieving financial success with a modest amount of additional income does not make us happier, and yet we continue to strive for more. We've bought into the illusion that doing more, harder, faster, and longer will help us reduce the discomfort of uncertainty.

So, we explain... often as a response to our own discomfort with uncertainty. Explaining is a way to manage perception, reduce ambiguity, and feel in control of something inherently uncontrollable: how others see us, how the future unfolds, and how the pieces eventually fit.

And whether we know it or want to admit it, many of us are control freaks. The only surprises we like are the ones we want. Because not knowing creates tension. Uncertainty feels uncomfortable. Surrender requires humility.

We live in a culture that celebrates explaining, being the one who "knows." Yet true wisdom so often comes from pausing in the performance of certainty. It's found in stillness, in the space between questions and answers.

Many of us, disliking this level of uncertainty, justify "working vacations" rather than surrender. This is often why transitions can be invaluable. Involuntary "still points"—whether a career pivot, an illness, or an extended work leave—force us to reset, change environments, and step away. In my own learning, I did two silent, fasting retreats. While I had "certainty" about what I was eating (nothing!), it forced me to be alone with myself, my thoughts, and my fears.

Detaching from work, family, and commitments felt so hard to do, and yet it offered more benefits than I could have anticipated. I was surprised that I was never bored or even hungry, but I missed the routine of meals. After a few days, the incessant internal chatter grew almost silent. I slept more deeply and needed less sleep to feel more rejuvenated. Rather than weak, I felt energized and excited to hike, run, and paddle. I could listen more deeply to myself. By day nine, I was surprised that I was longing for a few more days of solitude, stillness, and retreat. Ideally, I would do 4 days of silent, tech-free fasting each month but that is not Realistic now, with kids.

> ***Ideas —> Action***
>
> What myths have you seen or believed?
>
> What beliefs or expectations have you accepted as truths?

Life rarely offers us clean narratives. Growth is messy. Transitions are nonlinear. And sometimes the most powerful move is to say, "I don't know yet." As we open to life, we see that it's filled with more shades of gray than black and white. Rarely is anything certain.

Benefits of Realing

Remember Dave, the man whose stumble led to his Parkinson's diagnosis and significant life changes? In my opinion, Dave is an exceptional role model for making lemonade out of lemons. He felt the weight of his unexpected diagnosis but did not indulge in self-pity. He navigated through shattered illusions and clarified what matters. Then, he made the conscious choice to live more Real.

When we reconnected nearly five years later, he shared that he had never been happier. We celebrated the changes he'd made, and I discovered that his mindset shifts were truly awe-inspiring. He viewed his diagnosis as a gift—a clarifying really check about what mattered most. I was humbled to bear witness to his changed life, his new clarity, and ultimately his happiness.

After his diagnosis, Dave no longer wanted the pressure, stress, and distraction of being a CEO. Fortunately, as someone vital to his company, he was able to renegotiate his role, which resulted in less stress and travel. He spent more time with his family, prioritizing health and wellness. He reconnected to his body. He was so present and tuned in that he was able to notice small shifts that turned out to be due to leukemia. Cancer treatments seemed like a mere inconvenience for Dave. It was another challenge to juggle as he focused on living with even more love, connection, and compassion.

Laser clear on his commitments—to love his wife and four children—his Realing inspired those around him to be more Real. One of his children came out as gay, another transitioned, and Dave walked yet another down the aisle to marry the love of their life.

We shouldn't have to get a life-changing diagnosis to get clear on what really, really matters.

The Value of this Work

While going through tough times, it's common to want life to be better and easier. It's normal to wish the path were less winding and the road less bumpy. But after the fact, most people who've navigated any form of adversity appreciate what they've learned. While they do not wish it on anyone else, they see the value in who they have become as a result.

Just as there is no magic wand for fitness, there is no magic pill or genie-in-a-bottle moment when it comes to handling hard things. We will all have to face adversity, but how we choose to engage with it is what differentiates us. Embracing the lessons we learn is key. If we do not learn from our difficult moments and seasons in life, we gain nothing. You've undoubtedly heard it said that it's in the journey, not the destination, that we experience life to its fullest. Of course, that's true.

We are beginning to understand how important it is not to bypass life's precious moments. Mindfulness is vital. And when we use meditation to avoid hard things, it can bypass vital learnings and perspectives we might have gained. Embrace spiritual practices to cultivate more presence and to support us through these times. It is in the tension that consciousness is created, which moves us through it.

Our work is to face the fictional life scripts we have been sold about what a good life is. It's imperative we see the lies for what they are and choose a different path. This work requires the kind of honest seeing, courageous feeling, and intentional living that brings us back to ourselves. This is the work of Realing.

Three

Costs of Living Disconnected

Toxic positivity can unconsciously Shallow our existence, erode our relationships, and impede our well-being.

For too long, many of us have been told to look on the bright side, stay positive, and keep it together. Often unconsciously, we have learned not to engage with feelings, our own or those of others. Instead, we have been inducted into a culture of Shallow connections: a detached, disengaged, pleasant way of living where relationships remain superficial and suffering often goes unacknowledged.

While this may have seemed manageable—even comfortable for a time—we are now facing the stacking consequences. The cracks are widening. We see it in the overwhelm in our lives, in the escalating mental health crisis around us, and in the growing polarization and fragmentation of our communities. There's a collective ache of disconnection that's becoming harder to ignore. We are feeling the rising cost of living disconnected from our emotions, from our truth, and from one another.

To move toward change, we first have to name and feel the pain of this disconnection. We must understand what we have unintentionally sacrificed in our attempts to stay safe, to stay numb, to stay out of the messiness of feeling.

Only then can we begin the challenging—and deeply rewarding—work of Realing.

A Disconnected Moment

It can happen subtly, almost imperceptibly.

Nearly fifteen years ago, I attended a fortieth birthday party that still makes my heart ache. Friends, mostly moms, gathered at a restaurant to celebrate. I didn't know one of the women who had married a high school classmate of mine. Her name was Holly, and she was heavily pregnant with her third child and visibly distracted.

Amid the merrymaking, the stark reality of her story emerged: Holly and her husband had fought the night before, and he'd left her home alone with their two children. She didn't know where he'd gone or what he was doing, and she was worried.

I was struck by her raw vulnerability, and confused by how the others could simply go on to order yet another round of margaritas. I leaned in, deeply present to her suffering, genuinely curious how I could support her.

On the ride home, the birthday girl turned to me with a sharp finger, saying, "Do not pathologize this. Holly is just fine." With hindsight, I have come to appreciate that her response was less about Holly and more about her own discomfort and Shallowing.

In my sadness, there was also clarity. That day was hers—her birthday, her friends, and her rules. But the conversation with Holly and her friends' response gnawed at me for the days that followed, and I became even clearer about what I wanted in life. While I didn't know to call it this, I craved Realing. I wanted to be with people, like Holly, who were willing to be in the full range of feeling, being, and living. I do not wish adversity on anyone. However, when it arises, I want to be a place people turn to and to share and to be with all of life.

Although this was just one conversation from an evening long past, it still rings true for me in terms of the state of our lives and our desires. There is an accumulated cost or consequence when we choose to be safe, detached, and disconnected rather than compassionate, connected, and present.

I see this happening far too often: people muster the courage to come forward with something deeply distressing to them, only to be met with a wall of indifference or, worse, disapproval. Their glimmer of courage, of Realing, dissipates, and it can feel deeply personal. While Holly's "friends" were unable to see or hear through their own complex web of perception, their reaction left pregnant Holly struggling, feeling even more rejected.

That evening marked both the end of my relationship with the birthday girl and an awakening in my soul. I realized that I am someone who doesn't want to make things Shallow or simplify situations. Not only do I covet candor and compassion, but I also believe it's vital. I do not wish for the pretty, easy, packaged facade—I value what's Real.

That night helped me crystallize what I no longer wanted. I became keenly aware of the interactions that nourished me and how I want to engage in relationships. Authenticity and vulnerability felt essential for genuine connection, for Realing. Since that evening, through small shifts, I have more intentionally invested in these types of more fulfilling relationships.

Soul Suppression

Once we see how Shallowing shows up in our lives, we can no longer ignore it and what it's costing us—mentally, emotionally, relationally. The loss is subtle at first: a dullness, a disconnect, a sense of drifting. Over time, Shallowing becomes something more. We feel off, anxious, flattened. It can feel heavy. And we often do not know why.

It starts with a dulled connection to ourselves. When we don't have a clear sense of who we are or how we are meant to feel, we settle for less. We normalize the constriction. We accept a Shallowed version of life. What begins as numbing hard things starts stacking up, and we struggle to feel our emotions, to feel our bodies, and even to hear our own thoughts.

The long-term consequences of Shallowing can be profound. Emotional suppression is a coping mechanism sometimes used to maintain social harmony, navigate stress, or sidestep conflict. At times, it can appear as a strength—poise, professionalism, control. And to some extent, it is adaptive. We *do* need to function in the world. We *must* learn to regulate our responses. But when suppression becomes the default mode rather than an occasional strategy, it detaches or severs us from ourselves.

Years ago, I worked for the State Department in Africa as a refugee resettlement caseworker. In remote camps, I would document stories of persecution to determine immigration eligibility. Shallowing became a survival mechanism. One day, I found myself recounting one woman's story and asking for clarification. "So, you were raped eight times and had fourteen family members killed by the rebels. How many of those did you witness directly, and is your current pregnancy from one of these assaults?" I was horrified to see how I had detached her story from my own humanity. Some emotions, like anger or joy, are hardwired. Humans also have a unique capacity to manipulate or mute emotional expression in response to social norms. Politicians, professionals, and public figures are trained to keep their feelings out of sight. But most of us, in quieter ways, do the same thing. We swallow the lump in our throats at work. We smile when we want to cry. We downplay heartbreak because we don't want to seem vulnerable or fragile. And we do this not because we are broken, but because, somewhere along the line, we learned that honesty makes us unsafe or unappealing.

Long term, Shallowing is more than emotional suppression; it's soul suppression. This tendency is not new, but it is intensifying. We now live inside a cultural machinery that constantly reinforces emotional avoidance. The pressure to project a curated, high-achieving, aesthetically pristine life has never been higher. And it's not just external—it becomes internalized. We begin to Shallow our experience, and eventually, we start to shadow ourselves. Our digital lives accelerate this Shallowing. Social media amplifies the pressure, embedding it into our daily rhythms.

In 2023, the Pew Research Center reported that 31 percent of adults and over 50 percent of young adults (18-29) frequently feel anxious when they don't have their phone with them. Nomophobia, short for "no mobile phone phobia," is commonly associated with anxiety, irritability, disconnection, and boredom. Between 50-70 percent report feeling this in moderate ways, with 20-25 percent experiencing severe levels of anxiety coupled with physical symptoms of accelerated heart rate and perspiration.

Think about that. Nearly half of us experience physiological distress when disconnected from a device that did not even exist a generation ago.

Our bodies are responding as if we are under threat, not because we are weak, but because we have become disconnected from our internal world. We've grown so used to avoiding hard feelings that the mere prospect of being alone with our unfiltered thoughts triggers a nervous system response on par with encountering danger in the wild.

The cost of all this is profound. We are not just muting pain; we are muting life. The same wiring that numbs grief also numbs joy. The same reflex that avoids vulnerability also blocks connection. In trying so hard to maintain a polished, painless version of life, we end up forfeiting the raw, honest, beautiful truth of life.

But this is not the end of the story. Recognizing this pattern is the first act of liberation. Naming it makes space for something more profound. A return. A remembering. A way back to ourselves.

The Mental Health Epidemic

We are living in a mental health epidemic. Our collective mental health is fracturing under the weight of being disingenuously hyperconnected. The data tell a sobering story of how this Shallowing has eroded our psychological well-being. According to the Centers for Disease Control, nearly one in five American adults—52.9 million people—lived with diagnosable mental illness in 2020. More troubling still, only 46.2 percent received treatment. Depression rates tripled during the pandemic years, with young adults showing the steepest decline in psychological well-being.

The data captures the clinical manifestations of people who are Shallowed, disconnected, and disengaged.

The Burnout Epidemic

We are living in a burnout epidemic with alarming statistics: 59 percent of American workers report symptoms. The economic impact is staggering—workplace stress costs approximately $650 billion annually in lost productivity and stands as a primary driver of employee turnover across industries. Burnout cases increased by 33 percent from 2010 to 2020. There is no denying the problem.

Burnout is emotional, mental, and physical exhaustion caused by prolonged stress, overwhelm, or chronic imbalance between demands and resources. It manifests as detachment, reduced motivation, and a diminished sense of accomplishment or effectiveness.

It's easy to dismiss burnout—to revert to outdated definitions as an individual's failure to manage chronic stress. This misses the deeper reality.

Burnout is absolutely fueled by changing demographic trends—technological overload, increased job demands, and the "always on" culture. The pandemic accelerated this crisis, with 79 percent of employees experiencing work-related stress in a single month, according to the American Psychological Association's 2021 Work and Well-being Survey. At its core, burnout is the manifestation of disconnection, lack of purpose, and an inability to experience presence.

Yet the skyrocketing burnout rates reveal something else quite concerning: the long-term cost of Shallowing. This epidemic emerges from the interaction of chronic stress (living in an activated state) while simultaneously believing others are thriving, having fewer genuine connections, and possessing limited strategies to feel deeply.

> ### *Ideas —> Action*
> Where do you see people experiencing burnout?
> How does burnout show up in your life?

There's an energetic cost to stuffing grief, sadness, and disappointment into our metaphoric basements. Not only does our basement become full, but we lose access to our metaphoric second floor, which is where we are supposed to be keeping the essential activities for renewal, recharge, and restoration.

Rachel was a nurse who had risen through the ranks to become COO of a community hospital that served a low-income and underinsured community. Many people did not seek out medical help until illnesses advanced and there was an extreme need. During the pandemic, her stakeholders were at higher risk as frontline providers.

Rachel thrived in crises and gave her work everything. Initially, this involved establishing new safety procedures, testing facilities, and then vaccinations. As Covid eased up, she started to see how burned out she had become, and how much she had Shallowed. No amount of rest could re-energize her. She planned walks with friends, enjoyed dinners out with her husband, and even renovated her kitchen, in hopes of feeling herself again. It was only when her mother died unexpectedly that she saw how much she had sacrificed and how desperately she needed to make a change.

The Loneliness Epidemic: Connected Yet Isolated

We are living in a loneliness epidemic, with nearly 47 percent of American adults reporting feelings of isolation, while 43 percent say their relationships lack meaningful depth. Similar loneliness trends appear across the UK and Australia. Compounding these problems, many suffer in silence, too embarrassed to admit their isolation.

It's tempting to blame technology and social media, increased urbanization, mobility (people moving frequently), or the societal shift toward individualism. Yet each of these trends points to a singular underlying issue: the erosion of genuine, deep, interpersonal connections.

I encounter many people who consider themselves deeply connected online and believe they have friends, yet when asked who they would call in an emergency, they struggle to name someone, let alone to know their phone number. This digital facade of connection masks a profound disconnection—people who are surrounded by interactions, but starved for intimacy.

> ***Ideas —> Action***
> Where do you feel burnout, loneliness, depressed or anxious?
> What could help you forge deeper connection with others?

Depression and Anxiety: A Rising Tide

In 2022, 21.4 percent of American adults experienced symptoms of depression within a two-week period, while 18.2 percent reported anxiety symptoms during the same timeframe[1]. Even more alarming is the shift in well-being among young people. Depression rates for adolescents (ages 12 to 17) increased by 52 percent from 2005 to 2017. For young adults (ages 18 to 25), rates rose by 63 percent between 2009 and 2017.[2]

Like the trends driving increased loneliness, rising rates of depression and anxiety reflect digital, cultural, and global

---

[1] Terlizzi, E. P., & Zablotsky, B. (2024). *Symptoms of Anxiety and Depression Among Adults: United States, 2019 and 2022.* National Health Statistics Reports, (213). Centers for Disease Control and Prevention.

[2] Twenge, J. M., Cooper, A. B., Joiner, T. E., Duffy, M. E., & Binau, S. G. (2019). *Age, Period, and Cohort Trends in Mood Disorder Indicators and Suicide-Related Outcomes in a Nationally Representative Dataset, 2005—2017.* Journal of Abnormal Psychology, 128(3), 185—199.

shifts. I believe our mental health epidemic is a stacking consequence of our collective resistance to being present, to feeling, and to processing hard things. These statistics reveal the cumulative impact of years—and generations—of Shallowing and stuffing difficult emotions into the metaphoric basement of our consciousness.

Rather than place blame, this is a call to Real. The path forward is not through more distractions or surface-level solutions; it is by mastering the mindset needed to be more present, by creating genuine and heartfelt connections, and by allowing ourselves to feel fully.

Even our therapists and counselors are exhausted. And still, the conventional approaches are not enough. We need a fundamental shift in how we relate to ourselves, to one another, and to the inevitable difficulties that arise in human existence.

Overwired, Overtired, and Disengaged

In my first book, *Rewired* (2011), I captured how technology is changing us. With "everything" at our fingertips, we are more digitally connected, yet less emotionally connected. The ease of technology makes it easy to be overwired as part of feeling productive. The 24/7 nature of countless channels and platforms makes it easier to distract, numb, and Shallow.

We are ill-prepared to toggle between the stimuli of life (genuine relationships, feelings, and challenging things) and the stimuli online (easy, accessible, engaging, and distracting). Being always on, always connected, not only leaves us feeling overwired and overtired, but it also "rewards" us for Shallowing. While we might recognize our addiction to living always on, always connected, fewer recognize the costs and consequences.

Externally, we are also being pulled away from ourselves. With a cracked internal compass, we have looked outward to define how we should feel and what we should want. Social media filled the void, became our mirror, reflecting a curated "good life" that we are told to desire. We scroll through glossy images, subconsciously aligning ourselves with lives that are staged, filtered, and ultimately hollow. And in doing so, we disconnect from the more profound truth of our own experience.

Instead of moving inward, we chase external illusions. Instead of discerning what matters, we accept projections of what others say will make us happy. Instead of listening inward, we try to emulate someone else's highlight reel. But true well-being will never be found in mimicry. It lives in individuation.

> ***Ideas —> Action***
> When's the last time you fully disconnected from outside distractions?

Reconnecting

We crave feeling alive—that state of being in flow, integrated, and purposeful. Flow occurs when the head, heart, and body align and work together. In these moments, questions of capability vanish. We feel nourished, whole, and vibrant with our life force.

Too often, we settle for the opposite of flow: being disconnected. We bifurcate our head from our heart and body, leaving ourselves disconnected from our feelings, our well-being, and our inner knowing. Leaving us feeling less alive.

One way we disconnect is when we take actions that feel incongruent with our values, beliefs, or emotions. Psychologists call this cognitive dissonance. We surf the web when we know we really need a walk. We have another drink, when we see that what we really need is sleep. We look online at what the Joneses are doing, when we should tend to our own family. We disconnect from ourselves, our wisdom, and our well-being.

By now, perhaps you've glimpsed this pattern in yourself. You've felt the costs of living Shallow. But cognitive understanding alone falls short—we need to understand emotionally that a great life is a whole, connected life, so that it resonates at a deeper level.

The perception that life should be easy has left scars. For some, disconnecting has atrophied their capacity to feel. Others have lost access to their full emotional range.

Science increasingly reveals that knowing is not purely cognitive, logical, or cerebral. A highly trained scientist would struggle to differentiate between a brain cell and a gut cell, suggesting that "gut feel" or "gut knowing" is quite literal. When we disconnect head and heart from body, we shut down our wisdom, intuition, and inner knowing. This disconnection diminishes our creativity, joy, fulfillment, and capacity to live at our fullest potential.

Remember, each of us contains depths most never see. The moment I began to truly listen and witness people in their raw authenticity, I appreciated them on a deeper level. I was amazed by the texture and complexity beneath every surface.

Soul Dysmorphia

As we move toward a more Real, integrated, and connected existence, consider the parallel with eating disorders. Individuals suffering from bulimia or anorexia often experience body dysmorphia: a disconnect between the reality of their bodies and their lived, felt perception. They genuinely cannot feel within their bodies, seeing themselves only through a dysregulated filter. An eighty-pound withering individual may see excess weight through a warped lens.

I would argue that Shallowing creates a similar experience—what I term "soul dysmorphia." This is a fundamental disconnection between our inner world of beliefs, values, and aspirations, and our outer life, which includes social media presence, professional titles, and material possessions. Like those with eating disorders, we did not consciously choose this soul dysmorphia. We struggle to reclaim reality, to create a new, stable way of being.

> *[Def] Soul Dysmorphia: When one's external world is misaligned or discordant with one's internal beliefs, values or aspiration. Characterized by excessive attention or preoccupation with external image or perception at the expense of their internal well-being.*

The disparity becomes stark and actionable when we recognize how much energy we expend facing outward, obsessively scanning the external world, perpetually anxious about others' perceptions. We've pushed away so much of ourselves, parts we have judged, shamed, disowned, condemned, and ignored.

Unpacking the basement of our soul can feel both intense and immense. Yet it begins with a single step, a singular embrace, one movement forward. What I have discovered is that we don't need to understand everything hidden in that basement. We don't have to construct meaning, apply logic, justify what happened, or know why it was difficult. All we have to do is shatter the illusion of its nonexistence.

The profound act of feeling can emerge from something remarkably simple: sunlight breaking through after darkness, the sudden beauty of a flower unfurling its petals, a spontaneous act of kindness, or the gift of a warm smile. There's an exquisite simplicity in experiencing these small, beatific moments. They arrest us midstride, leaving us stilled with wonder and awe, filled with reverence for the elementary beauty of being. And just as we open to wonder and awe, just as we expand into all that surrounds us and all that is becoming, we discover an invitation to soften into all parts of ourselves at last.

The good news is that reconnection with our internal self is possible. The first step back from the brink of lost awareness is to acknowledge how we disconnected from ourselves in the first place. We need to identify how we lost track of the voice inside us and of what matters, and how we tuned out our biological feedback.

Here's how that happens. By prioritizing external outcomes and validation alone, we stop listening to our own truth, purpose, desires, and calling. We lose the longing to be seen, heard, valued, and recognized for who we are, apart from external accomplishments. In its purest form, Realing helps individuals reclaim their identity, to acknowledge they are *enough* and *worthy* of love.

A Way Forward

Too many of us received the message that to be loved or accepted, we had to be *less*. Less intense. Less emotional. Less Real. We learned to become more mild, more contained, more polished. We bought into the illusion that success was power, fame, and money. We became experts at packaging ourselves in ways that felt acceptable to the world around us—even when it meant betraying or disowning parts of who we truly are.

It takes courage to look in the mirror, to see hard things clearly, and to feel discomfort without numbing. Many people say they want to be more present, more connected, and more genuine, but they are unsure of how to do so. Realing is a lifelong process, a commitment to being present. Not a replacement for therapy, but rather a supplement. I invite you to Real with me, and the next chapter shows you how.

Four

An Invitation to Real

Full presence can create an awakening, an invocation to listen inward.

Every moment, you stand at a crossroads, you can stay Shallow or go Real. Shallow is easier in the short-term. It's surface-level conversations, scrolling, and avoiding. It's saying you're fine when you're not. It's life on autopilot: safe, predictable, but hollow.

Real is different. Real requires courage. It means looking at what's actually there—your emotions, patterns, fears, questions—without turning away. It's choosing depth in a world that encourages detachment. It's showing up for yourself, for others, for life in a way that is raw, true, and undeniably alive.

Shallowing is like floating on the surface of the ocean, afraid to dive down and never experiencing the beauty that lies in the depths.

A Shallow life never truly feels satisfying. You can only ignore your deeper self for so long before it starts feeling like you're missing something essential. Because you are. Awareness is an opening.

While people hire me for my coaching services, I'm actually in the business of presence. There's a quiet, decisive, unmistakable moment in my work where I witness the unlocking of a soul. After months or years of running on autopilot, striving, pushing, and achieving, something clicks in my clients when we connect. They feel seen, heard, and witnessed, like they are finally enough. It's the moment when someone remembers who they are. Their eyes soften. Their voice grounds. Their whole presence shifts, as if something essential has returned home.

My client Mira was longing for that return herself. A young executive and CEO, she had built her company from the ground up, leading a team of hundreds. By every external measure, she was succeeding brilliantly. But as we sat together, the weariness in her shoulders and the ache in her voice told a different story.

"I don't recognize myself anymore," she admitted quietly. "I used to love what I built. Now I feel like a firefighter, just managing the urgency of today."

Mira was living in a state of activation, where cortisol and adrenaline, two neurochemicals that fuel heightened alertness, kept her constantly ready for battle. Her body was tight, her breathing shallow. Each decision came from a place of reaction rather than creation. Every moment of her day was scheduled and spoken for. Her world narrowed to problems requiring immediate solutions.

I started asking Mira some hard questions, and together, we began a journey that led her back into her creative energy and joy.

I asked her, "What do you love doing when not at work?" She muttered, "You know, I don't know anymore... I don't know what I do outside of work and working out."

I probed deeper. "When you do have time, who do you like to spend it with?" I was met with a hollow stare. As I waited, her eyes welled with tears. The realization of just how empty her life was cracked something open.

Jumping back in time, I dug deeper. "What is it you loved to do as a child? Where would you completely lose track of time and space?" Suddenly, the floodgates opened.

As we returned to the present, she slowed down and listened inward. Her decisions began to flow from clarity rather than urgency, from intuition rather than logical cause and effect. Her body softened. Her vision widened. And her access to joy, once buried under obligation, began to rise again.

Mira was able to find the internal shift, a return to presence, a reawakening of creative energy, and a reminder that we do not have to live in a constant state of reaction. We can choose to come back to ourselves. We can Real.

Ask Hard Questions

As a business psychologist, I'm trained to help leaders engage in perspective-taking, stepping back to gain a clear view of what's really going on. This means I'm well-positioned to ask hard questions—the kind that force leaders to address issues just below the surface before those issues blow up.

Clients are usually laser-clear on their goals (the *what*), but I often find that they've failed to prioritize and honor the need for their internal preparation and growth (the who and how). Once they do that via Realing, the results transform every aspect of their lives. Of course, this is not always easy if you're used to an external rather than internal focus.

What I've found most beneficial for clients is for them to "gain altitude," as I like to call it, meaning taking a holistic approach to how they view their lives. Gaining altitude starts by sitting with the hard questions.

This is ultimately what opened John, the soccer athlete turned corporate victor. One day, as he was ticking through a recent successful acquisition, I asked if he felt happier now with this "win" under his belt. For longer than usual, he sat puzzled. Typically so focused on what he wanted, he was getting perspective, or altitude. Beyond wondering why he had wanted it so much in the first place, I could see him wrestling with what "happier" really felt like.

Together, we identify areas where they may lack presence, motivation, or development. We begin to bridge the concrete objectives in their career with how they are operating at home. Why? Because if things aren't working at work, chances are they aren't working in other areas as well.

I share this because it's in the act of Realing that breakthroughs happen, and I've seen it time and again during the twenty years of my coaching.

Think about this for a moment.

- When was the last time you sat with yourself and looked at everything in its fullness?
- Did you see that you weren't fully present at your child's sports game last weekend because you were checking emails?
- How about those moments at the dinner table, interrupted by your thoughts still being at work?

> **Ideas —>Action**
>
> Take time to reflect and journal on these questions. What small shifts well help you be more present? To see the fullness of life?

Asking hard questions is not about making you want to put down the book before you finish. It's about seeing things as they are. Realing with a trusted friend can make this easier. Visit LivingReal.AIMleadership.com to connect with others on this path. Being honest with yourself is one of the most brutal (and loving) acts of vulnerability you can offer yourself. You know somewhere inside it, in these moments of truth, you will find resolve.

There is a collective longing to feel more enlivened. We crave feeling fully alive in the moment and aligned in our actions. This is not bashing success. You can be successful, at the top of your game, and still be Realing. We can be successful, present, and happy, simultaneously. This is enlivenment and the promise of *Living Real*.

> *[DEF] Enlivened: The ways we feel energized, aligned, and integrated when living Real and accessing our whole self, operating from self-renewing energy when inner truth and outer expression align. When you feel more yourself fully and more present.*

How did I get here? you ask yourself. *I've worked so hard. I did everything right!*

Yes, you did everything you were told to do. The degree, the career, the partner, the home, the family. You've cultivated the perfect marriage, home, and family life, and have picture-perfect vacation photos scattered throughout your home and office to prove it. From the outside, everything says you've succeeded. Yet in moments of quiet reflection lying awake at 3:00 a.m., you think, *Is this it? Is this all in my life? Isn't there something more?*

You are not alone in feeling this way. I see this life pattern in high achievers every day. And I can tell you unequivocally, the answer is: Yes, there is more. More depth, more vibrancy, more fulfillment—but only if you begin to wake up to it.

All Compassion Starts with Self-Compassion

Until now, we have been exploring what it means to be Shallow and Real. We need to understand where we are, why it's not working, and how we got here, so we can change.

My beloved Uncle Phil was quirky and stubborn, but he never missed an opportunity to connect, be present, and focus on what mattered. This is one of the traits I miss the most. Anticipating our Thanksgiving visit, he would strategically work in the woods, drag brush into a big pile in a field close enough for my young kids to hike to after dinner but far enough that it felt like a quest. He would watch the weather, often walking to cover this pile with big tarps if rain was approaching. He would delight in the ensuing bonfire. With him, time stilled. It was easier to exhale and listen inward in his full presence by the crackling fire. He reminded me that the quality of our presence always trumps the quantity of time.

We yearn to be seen. We yearn for meaningful connection. We yearn to be accepted. Realing permits us to do all of this.

Permission to Stop

You can stop. You can breathe out, exhaling all the shoulds. You can take a breath in. You can start to feel inward. You can begin to listen inward. And, if you can linger long enough, you can start to hear yourself.

We keep so much of our life scheduled, structured, and controlled. We are so focused on the future, that we often don't know what lies within ourselves. Sometimes, doing nothing is the most significant and courageous action, whether it's for an afternoon, a weekend, or a month.

Permission to Let Go

Letting go is not reckless abandonment. It's discerning what no longer serves us and releasing it. It's stepping forward into uncertainty.

Just like you might thin out a closet of outdated clothes that no longer fit, let some things go. Let go of things that are taking up emotional space and abusing your psychological Real estate. Prune outgrown assumptions and narratives to allow new possibilities to flourish.

Permission to Be Still

We are so conditioned to the constant motion of our lives that stillness often feels unfamiliar and untethering.

Be still. Shed the noise of frenetic doing and step into being, feeling, and hearing. Create space for yourself to breathe, to dream.

Neurologically, stillness is essential. Our brains need quiet to integrate and make sense of our experiences. Without it, we process information superficially, miss deeper patterns, and overlook the exact connections that can lead us to genuine insight.

Permission to Listen Inward

For most of our lives, we have focused on listening outward to instructions, expectations, and feedback. We're told who to be, how to act, and what to do next. Rarely are we invited to listen inward.

Finding stillness is a great way to tune into a different frequency. Much like you might settle into a meditation, listening inward begins by tuning into everything happening in and around you. Tuning into what is emanating from within you.

We typically listen at the surface, in a unidimensional way—hearing words but missing the vibrations. We catch the content but miss the larger context. However, when we begin practicing intentional listening, we can attune to its different layers and levels. This, in turn, expands our aperture of awareness both internally and externally. We begin to perceive the world through fresh dimensions of sound, vibration, and information that were previously inaccessible to us.

Expanding your capacity for dimensional listening, finding space for stillness, and tuning your awareness to what is happening around you are essential to practices. Notice the environmental sounds around you. This could be the buzz of a heater, the rumble of a truck, or the birds. Next, notice the internal noise within you. This often can feel like the gurgling of shoulds or to-dos, beckoning your attention.

If you can stay still, there is often a gateway to inner listening. What do you hear beyond the layered complexity of your surroundings and your inner voice? Allow your capacity to listen outward in the world and to listen inward. You might be surprised by what you finally hear within yourself with practice.

Permission to Be Uncertain

We're used to being celebrated for taking decisive action and providing quick answers. We've been conditioned to offer immediate solutions, to project control, certainty, and a sense of knowing. Realing is an invitation to surrender control. To hold the tension of multiple correct responses. Acknowledging uncertainty and duality opens us up to possibilities beyond our current understanding.

The practice of deep listening requires a willingness to set aside what you know. We receive information differently when we listen with an empty cup rather than one already filled with preconceptions. Our nervous systems relax. Our defenses soften. We become receptive to nuance and complexity that our certainty would have filtered out.

Try not knowing. What might change in your leadership, relationships, and self-understanding if you approach each day with permission to not know? What possibilities might emerge in that spacious uncertainty?

Consider how different conversations might unfold when you approach them without demonstrating your expertise. Could questions become genuine inquiries, rather than setups for displaying your knowledge? Could pauses become opportunities for reflection rather than uncomfortable gaps to fill?

> **Ideas —> Action**
>
> Give yourself permission.
>
> Where do you need to give yourself permission?
>
> To end something? To let go of something? To begin something new? To just be, in stillness?

Your Realing Journey Is Unique

If what you've read so far lands deep, and if you feel the quiet sting of recognition, I want you to know: I see you. And I'm both thrilled and sorry. Because once the veil lifts and you start seeing the patterns of Shallowing, you cannot unsee it. It's everywhere.

You'll hear it in the small talk that avoids tenderness. You'll feel it in how people shift away from the truth, even when it is begging to be spoken. You'll notice how often we reach for distraction instead of presence, performance instead of intimacy. You'll feel the ache of what's been lost in the name of staying comfortable. And that's when the real work begins. The work of choosing depth, again and again, in a world that rewards the surface.

Your Realing journey is yours alone. Maybe you already know how avoidance shaped your story. Maybe you've felt the cost in your bones. If so, you don't need a recap, but a way forward. This book is here to meet you in motion.

Start where you are. Skip ahead if you need (Chapter 5 is waiting). But wherever you begin, stay gentle with yourself. Compassion is the groundwork. And yes, it will take effort.

Think of it as less like peeling an onion and more like working through an artichoke. Those tough outer leaves, those defenses, they have their place. They've kept you safe. But what lives at the center, that tender, genuine, wildly alive part of you, is worth every layer.

Activate Your New Insights From Part 1

You understand the cost of shallowing, the lies we've believed, and the impact of living disconnected. You are ready to live more Real.

To help you implement these ideas, we've created quick, focused exercises to help you move from awareness to action.

Scan this QR code to access reflection prompts, integration tools, or download our mobile app so you can stay connected to what matters most and engage support.

PART II

THE OPPORTUNITY TO REAL

Now that we understand the difference between Shallowing and Realing, including how we got here and why we may resort to living a less than whole existence, we are ready to shift. The next section shares mindsets that will help you live more fully present in all of life, in its rawness. This book is not a panacea, but rather what I hope will be a gateway to help you be more present.

Recap: Life as a Sine Wave

When I lost my grandmother, my grief formed a valley as deep as the peaks of our love. This symmetry reveals a fundamental truth: the depth of our pain directly reflects the height of our connection. Our emotions do not operate on separate tracks, but as complementary expressions of the same wave.

Truly living means embracing the complete wave—both the exhilarating crests and the devastating troughs.

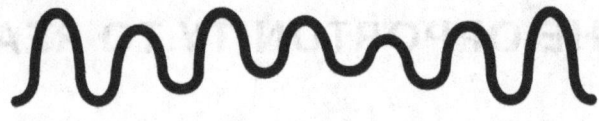

Realing is experiencing the full range of life.
Highs of Life

Lows of Life

[DEF] To Real: To be present and engaged in the full range of life. To see things as they are, to stay present in the both/and, and to feel fully the raw, unfiltered, and authentic. To resist the urge to Shallow, numb, or dismiss challenging experiences.

Recap: The House Metaphor

When you routinely stuff complicated feelings into your mental basement, you initially create a clean, simple life on the first floor. However, for each box in the basement, there is a parallel box that blocks space on the second floor. Over time, as the basement fills up, it eventually erodes our capacity to be present.

Each time you refuse to feel the lows of life; you limit your ability to reach the highs. Your emotional range becomes compressed, and you're left hovering at the edges of your own experience.

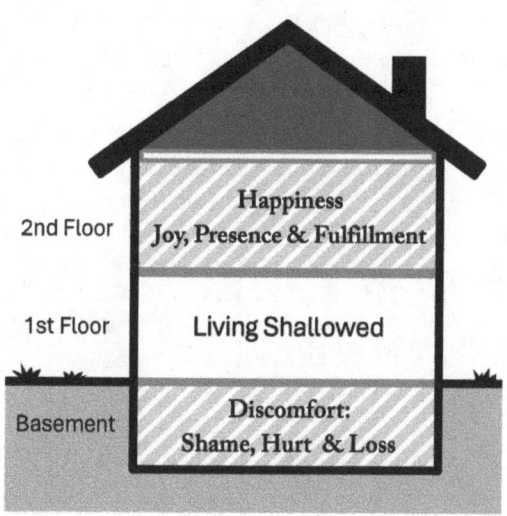

Living Real is an invitation to reclaim who you are, what matters most, and how you want to live to be more present and have fewer regrets. It's a form of soul honesty that creates alignment between who you are and how you live. Realing is what happens when truth meets courage inside a human body. And it begins to change everything.

Five

Embracing Both/And

Everything can change in a moment.

Realing is a surrender to adopting new mindsets, ones that help us see the full truth. It requires an admission that life is uncertain, that we don't know and can't control the future. It recognizes that life is far more complex than the series of simple black-and-white answers we have relied upon.

Embracing both/and—instead of either/or—is a gateway to being present. Rather than retreating into certainty or rigidity, both/and invites us to stay with what is. It helps us holds on to the now, especially when it is complex or contrasting.

You Have a Different Child

While living in Doha, Qatar, my friend Alice experienced what I can only imagine is every parent's worst nightmare.

Her three-year-old son was not well, and when she took him to the hospital, she was quickly dismissed as a "crazy white woman." Doctor after doctor shamed her, telling her she was overreacting. She knew in her bones that they were wrong with a deep certainty that mothers carry, in a way that transcends medical training. And when they eventually sent her home, she also knew that she was powerless to do anything about it at that moment.

Less than forty-eight hours later, she was back in the hospital, with her son in a near coma, where she demanded to speak with the chief medical officer. Seeing her son's condition, the doctors jumped quickly into action and ran extensive tests that led to his diagnosis of Type 1 diabetes.

Needless to say, it was a traumatic weekend, and one filled with heartbreak, anger, and the realization of what the diabetes diagnosis meant. As she learned how to draw blood, interpret results, calculate insulin, administer shots, and rethink food as she knew it, she faced the harsh reality of what their new life would be like in the years ahead.

A Canadian doctor on duty that weekend pulled her aside and said something along the lines of, "I'm really glad your son is doing better. And I'm sorry that you had this hard time.

I know you're focused on learning and mastering everything you can about diabetes and all of the details you'll need to know for his care. And since you're staying in the hospital with him for the next few days, I want to encourage you to take some time to take care of yourself. I know it might not have sunk in yet, but you're going home with a very different child than you brought in. And you are going home to a very different future than you had anticipated. You must take time to feel the full range of emotions associated with the changes that are happening and the changes ahead."

What a brilliant doctor. He recognized her transition, naming what was happening, and then, like my father, encouraged her to feel. He effectively framed what it would mean for her to feel the full range of emotions. It was as if he took a flashlight and pointed out where she should focus—on medical knowledge and her own experience, too—and to look here and here. By illuminating the changes, he essentially invited her to take space and not to Shallow her emotions. He was inviting her to build Real intelligence.

When we focus on what needs to happen and the logic of those actions, we short-circuit or Shallow our own full range of awareness of the situation. In our busyness, we miss opportunities to curate Real intelligence. As a protective mama bear, she wanted to understand everything she could so she could serve her son at the highest level. In a single weekend, she became a lawyer turned medical student, trying to understand everything there was to know about her son's disease. She was both the mom who wanted to do everything for her son and the woman whose life had changed forever.

What that Canadian doctor offered Alice was not just medical advice—it was Realing. He gave her permission to be present and embrace the fullness of her new truth, something we often resist. When something at a person's core breaks, it must be held with reverence and love. There is a surrender and acceptance before we can fully understand the transition and what is becoming.

Remember kintsugi, the Japanese art of repairing broken pottery with gold? Instead of hiding away our breaks or discarding what's broken, we can celebrate our fractures. When "repaired" in this way, our broken places become gold-filled seams that become our most striking feature, not as a flaw to conceal but as a testament to our resilience.

When reality shatters our assumptions about life, as it did for Alice that day in the hospital, we are left with broken pieces that do not resemble our preconceived notions of what our lives would look like. Society often tells us to hide those breaks and to present ourselves as resilient and unscathed, as if we are intact and life hasn't marked us. However, this pursuit of an unblemished existence is deeply flawed because *it is impossible*. The broken pottery will never be the same, but it contains its own unique strength and beauty.

Whatever our unique circumstances and identity, the truth of our breaking will unfold in three stages, which may occur quickly or take years (or maybe decades) to complete.

> ***Ideas —> Action***
>
> How can you start to lean into this concept of Both/And?
>
> Where is there tension that needs to be explored?
>
> How can you reframe this current situation to see beyond it?

Learning to Embrace Both/And

Joy cannot exist without sorrow; deep laughter requires the capacity for tears. True embodiment means embracing this totality with full presence and awareness. Being present to it all is both challenging and vital. It is only when we can be in the tension, the both/and, that we can open to greater consciousness.

Realing is like a gym workout: when we do hard things, we push against resistance, we make microtears in our muscles that are vital to our growth. Hard things make us stronger. When we sit with discomfort rather than fleeing from it, we discover a gateway to freedom. When we learn to hold the tension, the both/and, the good and the bad, we are Real.

This truth crystallized for me recently at my kid's soccer game. Following a season marked by death, I was standing on the sidelines, feeling hot and overtired, and wondering how much time was left. A fellow parent, Haseem, asked how I was doing, and instead of saying "Fine," or "I'm okay," instead of Shallowing, I decided to Real.

"I'm exhausted," I said. "I flew in from a business trip late last night, my husband has the flu, this is my second soccer game of the day—after two lacrosse practices this morning—and well, it's just been a rough year. Honestly, this is the last place I want to be right now. I'm trying to enjoy the sunshine and plan our afternoon, but I just want to crawl into bed!"

Haseem's entire demeanor shifted. He went from hunched over with his arms folded to gesticulating enthusiastically, his eyebrows lifted. "Me too! Oh my god, I'm so, so tired.

My wife, Lauren, has been traveling back and forth to St. Louis, where she's caring for her mother. And now, she's realized just how advanced her father's dementia is. She's trying to figure out what to do for his long-term care and realized their finances are a mess. My work has been super demanding thanks to a recent merger, and I'm in charge of the kids now, too. I don't resent my wife, but it's a lot. I just want to order pizza, put on a movie, and collapse!"

For the rest of the game, Haseem and I sank into easy conversation—two parents on the sidelines, grateful to be Realing in real time. What began as a casual chat became something more: a moment of honest connection between two members of the so-called sandwich generation, quietly navigating aging parents, growing kids, and everything in between. This man, who had been little more than a familiar face after two years of our kids playing on the same team, suddenly felt like a friend. A fellow traveler.

With that one conversation, Haseem and I had intuitively created a kind of soccer bubble—a quiet, safe container where we could be genuine, messy, and open. Small enough to hold what mattered. Spacious enough to let us stay anchored in parenting, while still making room for presence and connection. Rather than negativity, Realing is speaking truth to what is. With Real Intelligence, we can metabolize the emotions and move forward with greater presence and happiness.

When we stop pretending that life should be easy and allow ourselves to name what's hard, we acknowledge the full spectrum of our experience. We do not just free ourselves. We create space for others to meet us there. To take off the mask. To get in the river, too. Because the Real treasure is not waiting on either shore. It's in the river, the current, the experience itself.

The Full Spectrum of Being Human

By now, I hope you've begun to recognize some part of yourself in this journey. Perhaps you've started to notice what it feels like to live just outside the Shallows. Maybe you're becoming more emotionally aware, more attuned to your rhythms, and more willing to feel what's Real.

I have come to appreciate that cognitive understanding can only take us so far. It's one thing to know something in your head. It is another to feel it in your bones.

That's why emotional intelligence matters. It is a vital part of reclaiming the full spectrum of our humanity. It helps us not only understand our emotions but navigate them so we can meet the world from a place of depth and alignment.

First introduced in the 1990s by Daniel Goleman, emotional intelligence (EQ) is the ability to be self-aware, to regulate our inner world, and to engage with others from a place of empathy and adaptability. It is a skillset that supports both resilience and connection, and while some of it is innate, much of it can be learned and strengthened over time.

What if EQ applied to living Real drives a new type of intelligence? Real intelligence (RQ) is when we can discern who we are, what matters most, and then craft a life that is more aligned. Sometimes this comes out of necessity, as with Dave and Alice. Other times it is an active choice, like Sam and Kea. Real intelligence is seeing the full range of the sine wave and then taking intentional action. It is clarifying and awe-inspiring to witness, and enlivening to experience.

[DEF] Real Intelligence: RQ is awareness about what is and our capacity to be. It is not about managing emotions into neat, digestible boxes. It is about honoring them as data, as direction, as doorways to deeper integration.

For some, refusing RQ has numbed their capacity to feel success, presence, and happiness. For others, it has narrowed their emotional range so much that even joy feels distant. For those who have learned to live entirely in their heads—cut off from their bodies and emotions—the ability to feel at all can feel entirely out of reach.

But what's been dulled can be reawakened. What's been Shallowed can be reclaimed. RQ gives us a way back to ourselves, to our aliveness, and to the kind of connection that makes life worth living.

Embrace the Messy Middle

Too often, we want to move from one side of the river of life to the other, to the place where we imagine ease, clarity, and authenticity. We long to leave behind what we now recognize as a Shallowed existence and step into something more honest, more alive. But we resist getting wet. We want to be present, but the i*n-between*—the river itself—feels uncomfortable, uncertain, and exposed.

I'm here to tell you that you have to get wet to learn how to swim. RQ is built through experiencing, not through thinking. Realing often begins right there: in the river. Not on the safe bank of certainty, and not yet on the other side. But in the messy, moving middle.

> *[DEF] The Messy Middle: The liminal, sacred space of being in-between. It is the stretch where you've said yes to growth, but haven't yet found solid ground. The space after the old ways of living becomes no longer enough, but before the new one arrives fully.*

When Alice first received her son's diagnosis, she was pulled into that middle without warning. One day, she was moving through life as usual, managing schedules, dreaming plans, holding a vision of how it was all supposed to go. Next, she was in unknown waters, grieving, questioning, navigating medical systems, and reshaping what motherhood would mean. She couldn't go back to who she was before. But she had no map for moving ahead.

And yet, in the middle of that river, even though she was fragile and aching, something deeper awakened. She educated herself, asked questions that terrified her, and made decisions without guarantees. Intuitively, she harnessed RQ. Eventually, she stopped fighting the current and learned to move with it. Not by bypassing her pain, but by allowing it to teach her. By letting herself feel the water as she crossed.

We eventually have to let go of the shore we have clung to—the old patterns, the outdated stories, the version of ourselves that knew how to survive but not how to feel. For so long, I didn't know how to read the river, let alone go with its current. I was focused on pushing the river. I had learned what I have come to call *forcing energy*. I was taught to "work hard" and pursue a "good life," often without considering the costs. I was rewarded for driving harder, striving faster, chasing the life I was told I should want. The titles. The milestones. The image of success.

But Realing is not about pushing. It's about allowing. It is about understanding all the forces at play. It's about being willing to feel the water, standing in the middle, and trusting. Crossing is not about force; it's about being present with a deeper source of energy. Realing engages us in feeling, aligning, and collaborating with ease.

Overflowing with *shoulds*, we often find ourselves unable to hear our own inner wants and desires. So focused on pushing the river of life forward, we barely notice the water rushing by. We miss the smooth rocks beneath our feet, the quiet power rising within us, the courage already coursing through our bodies, enlivening our souls.

Shedding the illusion of riverbanks of certainty and control, and allowing ourselves to be in the messy, chaotic river currents, can feel like everything we have packed away in the metaphorical house of our lives has spilled out. The boxes in the basement, the emotions we stored and forgot, the stories we hid from others and ourselves—suddenly, it's all out in the open.

And maybe, just maybe, that's precisely where it needs to be.

We do ourselves no favors by promoting the illusion that life is full of lollipops, sunshine, and rainbows. It's not about choosing one side of the river over the other. It's about being fully present wherever you are in the river, able to feel what's true in the moment while staying centered and grounded. The Messy Middle is where life happens. It's where we learn that happiness does not equal peace—it equals Real, and that is good.

The streaming series *Shrinking* is a sitcom built around three therapists, one of whom is estranged from his daughter and navigating Parkinson's, another who is navigating a divorce from a codependent addict, and a third who is recently widowed and trying to raise a hormonal teenage daughter. While the storylines are heightened for humor, what makes the show striking is how openly the characters say the quiet parts out loud—naming their discomfort, calling out social awkwardness, and exposing their inner contradictions.

It's funny, yes, but it's also deeply human. It is RQ. *Shrinking* offers a gently comic reminder that beneath the surface of our everyday routines, we are all carrying something. We're all trying, in our own messy ways, to find our way back to ourselves and each other. *Shrinking* does not shy away from the awkward or the unspoken—it holds it up to the light, reminding us that healing often begins when we stop pretending everything is fine.

We're taught to believe that success will bring happiness, peace, and uncomplicatedness.

I would argue that success is about being fully present—being able to feel it all, hold it all, and be present to it all (and sometimes that might be just for a short minute). Success is the capacity to remain grounded in your experience without needing to edit, sanitize, or perform it. It's knowing what you need at any given moment and having the courage to give it to yourself, or the vulnerability to ask others for support.

In *Shrinking*, we see this beautifully illustrated when a therapist, having recognized her friend's tendency toward Shallow emotional processing, doesn't judge or shame her. Instead, she compassionately teaches her exactly what she needs to do to be a good friend—how to show up authentically, how to hold space for complicated feelings, how to move beyond platitudes toward meaningful connection. This moment perfectly captures how we can deepen our emotional capacity through relationships with people who can see both where we are and where we might go.

People who've navigated the river, who have lived through hardship, share something surprising: Rarely would they give up what they learned from it. Ask someone who has experienced profound loss. They usually do not wish it away, because embedded in that difficulty was transformation that couldn't have come any other way.

Are you beginning to see the whole picture?

> ***Ideas —>Action***
>
> Reflecting on the river, what is in your Messy Middle?
>
> What is on the other side of the river?
>
> What needs attention or shifting in order to get there?

Individuation and the Messy Middle

When I first met Alice, I was struck by her intensity, but I had no idea what she was living through at the time. Looking back now, with age and perspective, I can see how quickly I imposed my own filters. I carried the quiet arrogance of my New England upbringing, unconsciously passing judgment without understanding the whole picture.

And I know I'm not alone in that. Most of us do this every day without realizing it. We absorb the assumptions of the world around us. We breathe in other people's beliefs and call them our own. We become shaped by our environments, complicit in the narratives we have inherited, often without ever pausing to question them.

At the time, I was unconscious of just how narrowly I saw others—and myself.

Alice and I met over 20 years ago at a Washington Sports Club. Tough as nails, she taught an intense early morning step class with weights. Her upbeat nature was matched by her energy as she was working out beside us, and often with heavier weights. In the locker room after class, as we readied for work, she would lament the trials of her ongoing divorce. I was quick to judge her thick Southern drawl, her enhanced bosom, and her impeccable outfits.

Despite our different upbringings, Alice and I were walking a shared path: each of us slowly stepping away from the lives we were told to want. Our parents were good people, loving, generous, but like all parents, they passed down their world views, their values, and their ideas of right and wrong.

What I remember most is watching Alice push up against the limits of the life that had been mapped out for her. Not through rebellion, but through a quiet, persistent way some people do when they are becoming. We were both in the process of shedding what no longer fit, and becoming who we were meant to be, not who we were expected to be.

Psychologists call this process individuation.

[DEF] Individuation: The lifelong process of becoming more fully yourself. The integration and acceptance of yourself (especially unconscious or Shallowed aspects) and your experiences into a more whole, balanced, and authentic self. It is often associated with separating from your family of origin.

Carl Jung described it as the lifelong journey of self-Realization, where we clarify our identity, deepen our self-awareness, and integrate the full spectrum of who we are. If we are courageous in our anti-Shallowing, we don't just shed roles and narratives; we illuminate the shadow. We accept what has been hidden, denied, or forgotten. And in doing so, we begin to live from a place of truth.

Individuation is not about perfection—it is an evolution that comes through integration. The work of becoming whole.

Over time, I learned that Alice was a fitness instructor in the mornings and a paralegal by day, as she was putting herself law school at night. She did not know exactly what she wanted to do long-term. She just knew that she did not want to stay in her small, South Carolina hometown and become an elementary school teacher like her mother and sister. She was willing to step away from everything she had known and into the Messy Middle of uncertainty.

Often, when someone presents as anxious, depressed, or emotionally flat, what's beneath the surface is a struggle to individuate. Sensitive to everything around them, they are seeking a sense of balance or ballast because they've lost connection to their inner reference point. Their identity is unstable, not because they are broken, but because they haven't yet found their true selves.

They often live lives shaped by external forces: overworking, overpleasing, and striving to meet invisible standards. They have become practiced at performance, but unpracticed at presence. And in the process, they lose sight of their own uniqueness—their texture, their voice, their essence.

Today, in a wired world of curated images and constant comparison, it is easy to be pulled off-center. We become externally referenced, measuring ourselves against someone else's definition of a good life. But individuation invites us back in. It invites us to slow down, to listen inward, to separate signals from noise. It reminds us that the goal is not to become someone better, but someone truer.

Six

Break the Cycle

Unconscious patterns become invisible chains.

To live more fully, we must build RQ to understand and intentionally break the loops of numbing, distraction, and overdoing. To disrupt the patterns, habits, and cycles that pull us away from presence, we must recognize them. While this happens at the individual, team, family, and organizational (community) levels, I strongly encourage you to start with yourself, on the personal, individual level.

Awareness as a Gateway

Kate engaged me just before starting what she hoped would be her dream job. She was enlivened and excited to work at a foundation that connected with the community and focused on issues that mattered deeply to her. In addition, this new job presented a tremendous growth opportunity and felt aligned with her longer-term career goals. She prepared diligently, and her eagerness was so marked that we were both equally surprised when Kate joined our Zoom call three weeks into the job and burst into tears.

While competent and committed, she was working harder than she could have anticipated. Together, we were fully present to her emotions with compassion and curiosity.

Kate had anticipated joining a dynamic, purpose-driven team to which she could contribute. Instead, she found herself on a treadmill fighting fires. Her new boss, the CEO, thrived on adrenaline, stress, and chaos. The CEO confused activated energy with impact and progress.

> *[DEF] Activated: Feeling heightened engagement and focus often as a result of a high-stress, high-pressure, high-stakes scenario. Cognitively engaged "logically" yet disconnected, frequently fueled by adrenaline and cortisol.*

While Kate was working in a well-intended organization, she found that the activation energy was so pervasive that her new peers were also in survival mode. She tried to enlist the aid of her work peers to help navigate her CEO's "crisis of the moment" mindset, but found her peers had already Shallowed. They had narrowed their focus to a transactional mindset based on immediate outcomes and did not want to collaborate. They had learned to detach, disengage, and Shallow at work to survive.

In her enthusiasm, Kate had initially embraced each new daily crisis. As priorities, targets, and deliverables constantly shifted during these daily debacles, Kate fell further behind. It was no wonder the emotions flowed when we were both fully present to her.

Whereas enlivened energy is more vital and integrated, activation energy is often results-driven and reliant on cortisol and adrenaline. Coupling adrenal fatigue with emotional suppression and detachment breeds the ideal environment for burnout. It was no wonder that three months into this role, determined to do well, drive results, and contribute, Kate was exhausted.

> *[DEF] Enlivened: Energy that comes from being integrated, aligned, and impactful. Feeling of focused engagement as a result of full presence and connection. Openness to complexity, the unknown, and growth. Often experienced in flow.*

Once Kate realized how much of her "failure" stemmed from the foundation's underdeveloped infrastructure, she could stop taking the situation personally and yet still be present and engaged. She was better equipped to depersonalize what had felt like rejection from her peers.

With perspective, she became curious about how to best implement solutions. She returned to the office with the ability to reconnect to her skills, core values, and strengths, as well as her deep desire to serve the community through the foundation. In other words, she was once again enlivened. Kate transitioned from the activated energy, which was more tied to burnout, to the enlivened energy associated with sustainability.

Altitude Is Essential for Perspective

In my coaching work, I introduce people to the concept of altitude. Like a helicopter, we can intentionally shift our perspective to see the same situation from different angles.

At ground level, the helicopter is immersed in detail. It sees the trees, the houses, and the life unfolding up close. It is deeply present in the moment, fully engaged with the world around it. But to gain perspective and to navigate effectively, we must rise up. We must lift into the sky, creating space between ourselves and the noise of the now. From this higher vantage point, we can see the whole landscape—where we have been, where we are, and where we are going.

> *[DEF] Altitude: It is the capacity to shift perspective to see differently. It is a mindset and skillset that helps us adapt to see either the bigger picture or the details while staying rooted in the moment.*

Altitude is vital to anti-Shallowing. When bad things happen that feel deeply personal or overwhelming, it can amplify our impulse to stuff or suppress emotions. We can manage the intensity by cultivating our ability to shift perspective or get altitude. When we can see and feel hard things from different angles, we can stay present. This builds RQ.

Altitude and presence are essential. They allow us to expand, orient toward what truly matters, rather than getting lost in the clutter of the present moment. We risk losing sight of ourselves when we stay too low for too long. We mistake proximity for truth. We accept what surrounds us as fixed reality rather than questioning, discerning, or imagining something different. At an altitude that is too low, we do not individuate—we simply inherit. We take what we have been told as fact.

The key is to start small and build awareness. I have witnessed the grief of two fathers who were widowed with younger children. While present to the depth of sorrow, they stayed at altitude to survive. One began his journey into Realing by dropping altitude and feeling the sadness fully, for twenty minutes a day. After he was sure his two toddlers were asleep, he would set a timer and let all the feels wash over him. He touched the raw emotions, surrendering control, softening into whatever it became.

Another father started Realing by surrendering twice a week to his grief during an acupuncture session. Away from his family and workplace, he felt safe and secluded, surrendering into all his emotions.

Having the right structures in place provides a framework to regulate and modulate our emotional experiences, helping us determine what we can process in a given period without triggering fight-or-flight responses. Many parts of Realing are complex, can feel abstract, and sometimes feel overwhelming. Through structure, these fathers built their capacity to hold grief. This container makes it safer to navigate the more challenging aspects of life.

> ***Ideas —> Action***
>
> What is your current altitude?
>
> Where do you need to change your altitude?
>
> Where could shifting perspectives help?

Identify Patterns

Patterns are the habits we form that impact the quality of our lives. Altitude helps us step back from the doing, shift our perspective, and then take intentional actions. Perspective is not given; it is intentionally created. From that space of higher clarity, we begin to see ourselves, our path, and what is possible.

In Chapter 1, we explored how our response to hard things is a pattern that drastically controls our actions and shapes the quality of our lives. Whether conscious or not, our ability to be Real or Shallow sets in motion a very different quality of relationship and presence.

Similarly, in Chapter 2, we uncovered the lies we had been sold and how these assumptions, beliefs, illusions, and hopes impact us and contribute to our behaviors. The more we understand and illuminate these patterns in our lives, the more conscious and intentional we can be in taking action, cultivating relationships, and designing the life we want.

Committing to being more Real, to anti-Shallowing, is a new behavior pattern. Just as Kate built her capacity to navigate her boss's stress, she learned not to become consumed by the crisis du jour.

As you become more present and Real, you will notice patterns in yourself and others that do not serve you. I urge you to write these down. Not everything can and needs to be solved now; awareness is the gateway to change. With awareness, we can explore both/and. We can recognize where patterns sometimes work and other times when they're destructive. With each awareness, we connect inward more deeply and open the possibility of hearing our inner wisdom.

> **Ideas —> Action**
>
> What are some of the patterns,
> habits or routines that you need to re-evaluate?
>
> What are you willing to change?

Differentiating Activated vs. Enlivened Energy

A big part of shifting from Shallow to Real is building awareness, recognizing patterns, and disrupting unhealthy cycles.

Although enlivened energy is more sustainable and scalable, we have been rewarded for forcing the energy of activation. Many of us consistently operate from an activated state. We're like engines running in the red zone—effective in short bursts, but unsustainable. Just like Shallowing, it's hard to understand the longer-term impact and sacrifices of stress, cortisol, and activation. It illuminates a different mindset.

Activated energy is like sugar: it acts in the short term, can be incredibly impactful, and might be deceptively addictive. It is the rush of being in crisis, the thrill of an affair, or the adrenaline of extreme sports.

Enlivened energy is more like vegetables or whole grains that require more preparation, alignment, and attention. It is the fulfillment of living your values, the contentment of being present, or the joy of a genuine, heartfelt conversation. Enlivened energy creates a longer-term fuel that is self-renewing and contributes to overall well-being.

Enlivened energy is self-renewing, holistic, and integrated. It's a way of being that feeds our soul, mind, body, and emotions. It embraces Realing and avoids emotional suppression. It's a depth of knowing and confidence that comes from being Real. While captivating, it's hard to understand enlivenment without experiencing it.

In writing this book, I reached back out to Kate, who was not only surviving but was thriving. She described the trust she had built with her still-chaotic boss through candor. Being new to the organization, Kate had a fresh perspective. She was able to get altitude, engage strategically, and identify both internal and external resistance. She witnessed how team members had over-personalized their boss's critique, and they struggled to detach. She could observe how their strong work ethic and desire to be of service became entwined in the organizational dysfunction.

Kate witnessed both the impact of Realing and all its layers. By first admitting to herself just how miserable she was, she was able to see work in a new way. That opened a gateway to her boss, then her peers, and ultimately, to serve the community. While not easy, she realized that it was more enlivening and fulfilling than she had anticipated.

> ***Ideas —> Action***
>
> Where do you see yourself being activated, using forcing energy?
>
> Where do you see yourself being enlivened, using sourcing energy?
>
> What would change if you slowed down?

Enlivenment Comes from Realing

Realing creates an upward spiral of energy and possibility. It's captivating like flow. The more we Real, the more we have the presence to feel the highs of life. More presence lets us see the whole situation, have more complete data, and make better decisions. The more we Real, the more skills, experience, and capacity we have to be with, feel, metabolize, and learn from hard things.

Practicing Realing feeds your soul, creating reserves for more challenging times. When my grandmother died, my father had presence for me because of his own practice. In the sadness of my uncle's death, I was fed and fueled by the times we had spent, the memories, and our love. I could replay the memories of time well spent, which soothed an aching heart.

In contrast, activated energy is more egoic, aggressive, and logical. It's cognitive, tactical, and analytical. It often engages a unidimensional short-term focus while overlooking systemic or indirect impacts. It is fueled by cortisol and adrenaline. While activated energy is invaluable in a crisis, overusing it is a way to Shallow—and detach or disengage from ourselves and those around us. It creates a rush that can be captivating while masking the longer-term costs.

We all want to feel. That's why some chase adrenaline—rock climbing, skydiving, heli-skiing, car racing at 200 mph—anything to stir sensation in a world that has grown Shallow and sterile. We see this with drugs and extra-marital relations. But I've witnessed something even more powerful: how the most hardened, closed-off souls begin to soften and bloom when they feel someone truly present with them. When we are seen—really seen—we come alive.

Recall Matt. Successful by all external metrics, he was often left wanting. Craving enlivenment, he pursued it through risky, short-lived moments of hyper-masculine conquests. As my friend Esther Perel recounts in her book, *The State of Affairs*, many people go outside their primary relationships to feel that enlivenment. Rather than signifying a bad relationship, cheating can reflect inner conflict. Seeking more enlivenment, infidelity appears as a gateway to novelty, autonomy, aliveness, or as a way to escape when one feels stuck, stagnant, or unfulfilled.

The external activity of always striving forward or maintaining a perfect image requires an intense and stressful level of energy. When this becomes our norm, we often numb and overlook the Real costs. Our body relies more on cortisol and adrenaline stress hormones, whereas enlivened energy is more vital and integrated.

Let me explain both the tensions and differences:

Activated Energy

- Feels aggressive, driven, and often forceful
- Primarily head-centered
- Runs on cortisol and adrenaline
- Tactical, logical, analytical
- Pursuing external metrics and validation
- Often unidimensional focus
- Depletes over time
- May feel like you are constantly chasing
- Tends to become addictive

Enlivened Energy

- Feels vital, integrated, flowing
- Incorporates head, heart, and body
- Sustainable biochemistry (balanced hormones)
- Intuitive, connected, resonant
- Guided by internal values and purpose
- Holistic, multidimensional
- Regenerative over time
- Can feel like you are being carried
- Tends to become self-reinforcing

There are long-term benefits of engaging from presence and alignment. Often, we mistake activation for enlivenment.

We are positively reinforced for intensity and learn to regulate the cortisol and adrenaline surges. Too often, we do not know how to differentiate, let alone access, the different energies. While we want to motivate ourselves holistically, we are so accustomed to operating in an activated state that we don't know how to listen to our inner selves.

Matt was so good under pressure that he enjoyed high-stakes, high-stress situations where he could shine. With cortisol and adrenaline surging, he became even clearer, focused, and decisive. Only when he was elevated into the c-suite did he start to see the unintended consequences of these deals to him, his team, and their relationships. As he understood the cost of these addictive patterns, he worked to develop new modes of being as fully engaged. The more he connected with *why* things were essential and *how* they impacted others, the more integrated and enlivened Matt became.

When we believe that success and happiness come from accomplishments, we are all the more likely to harness the energy of stress and the relentless push forward. As we Real, we reconnect our thoughts with our feelings and body. We start to feel, listen, and hear ourselves. And if we're lucky, we understand our desperate desire to just be. Fully present, in all that is, now.

Many of us are more addicted to stress hormones than we want to admit. The cortisol surge of a packed schedule and the adrenaline rush of racing deadlines can create a biochemical high that feels important, feels like impact. This physiological cascade becomes evidence that we matter. But living in this overextended high can eventually lead to severe health conditions.

I've witnessed this type of cortisol-based leadership many times over the years. Each leader thinks that they have mastered the chaos, are admired for their eighty-hour workweeks, and that their grit will be rewarded. Many later find themselves crashing as their bodies start shutting down and relationships dwindle, and for what? Is it worth it in the end?

Studies show that repeated cortisol exposure causes the brain to adapt by down-regulating receptors and altering neural circuits in ways that parallel the development of drug tolerance. When stress-addicted individuals slow down, they often experience symptoms similar to substance withdrawal: irritability, anxiety, difficulty concentrating, sleep disturbances, and intense cravings for stimulation. They may suffer sleepless nights despite the fact that everything is going well.

Chronically elevated cortisol levels from persistent activation can lead to these impairments:

- Impaired cognitive function (especially creativity and strategic thinking)
- Suppressed immune function
- Disrupted sleep patterns
- Muscle breakdown
- Increased inflammation
- Reduced capacity for empathy and connection

Armed with only anecdotal evidence, these are the same symptoms of Shallowed individuals. When we operate primarily in activation mode, we borrow energy from our future selves.

It's like constantly overdrawing from our energy account—at some point, the debt must be repaid, often with significant interest in illness, relationship breakdown, or burnout.

The distinction between activation and enlivenment is neurobiological and philosophical. Researchers have identified distinct neural patterns associated with these different states of engagement. Activation tends to trigger our sympathetic nervous system—the fight-or-flight response—narrowing our focus, increasing vigilance, and mobilizing quick energy resources. While useful for immediate challenges, this state limits access to our brain's most sophisticated capacities.

In contrast, enlivenment balances our sympathetic and parasympathetic systems—what some researchers call "flow state" or "challenge and connection." In this state, we remain energized but not reactive, focused yet flexible, and engaged without being consumed.

> ### *Ideas —> Action*
> Reflect back to the lists of activated and enlivened energy.
>
> Which of these symptoms do you see in others?
>
> Which do you see in yourself?
>
> What drives these ways of being?

Neuroimaging studies show that in a more balanced or enlivened state, we experience the following:

- Increased activity in the prefrontal cortex (supporting complex problem-solving)
- Enhanced connectivity between brain regions (enabling creative integration)
- Optimal levels of neurotransmitters like dopamine (supporting motivation without addictive cycles)
- Regulated stress response (providing energy without depleting resources)

When we operate from enlivenment rather than activation, we access our full cognitive and emotional capabilities. We make better decisions, connect more authentically with others, and sustain our energy for the long term.

Like Kate's CEO, many of us have become addicted to the neurochemical cocktail of stress. The adrenaline rush of urgency, the dopamine hit of checking items off a list, the cortisol surge that keeps us vigilant create a cycle that, while depleting, can feel oddly satisfying and familiar.

Just like Realing, breaking this addiction requires both awareness and alternative experiences. With altitude, we recognize our reliance on stress chemistry and invest in creating opportunities to experience the distinct and ultimately more fulfilling state of enlivenment.

Here's what this looks like in practice:

- Notice when you are "stress-seeking"—creating artificial urgency to feel good.
- Invest in experiencing alternative states—moments of flow, genuine connection, and natural joy.
- Resist the urge to overschedule—create space for stillness, integration, and emergence.
- Seek out and surround yourself with people who operate more from a state of enlivenment rather than constant activation.
- Sit in the tension and discomfort of slowing down or shifting focus.
- Cultivate patience with the transition—neural pathways take time to repattern.

Like Kate, many of us face challenging situations that make it impossible to succeed. Getting altitude helps us to see how we have been wired, rewarded, and reinforced for living activated. Building RQ, we are more able to identify and disrupt these cycles. With perspective, we experience with more candor. We differentiate ourselves from the patterns we have adopted unconsciously. We notice when others are fueled by stress and activation, and we can calibrate to stay more present and enlivened. Breaking these cycles both creates tension and opens us to new ways of being and deeper awareness.

Seven

Hold The Tension

Fostering your capacity to be present amid complexity and discomfort is the greatest path to consciousness.

Time and again, I have witnessed how tension creates consciousness. When we can stay present during difficult times, we can expand our capacity to handle them. We become more whole when we resist the urge to Shallow or numb. Tension, when held, can become a catalyst for new possibilities and new ways of being. Seeing differently, feeling more deeply, and living more truthfully.

Realing gives us an immense opportunity to hold tension and grow. Not for the faint of heart, Realing beckons us to feel the highs and the lows. Be with clarity and confusion. Sit in both the light and the dark. It demands that we hold the both/and—the polarities, the paradoxes, the Messy Middle—while staying engaged.

It is about being present to it all with deep compassion. The more we can ask hard questions and listen with curiosity to the uncomfortable truths, the more we can resist judging, jumping into action, and trying to fix things. When we can sit in discomfort and embrace hard things, we become more present. We build our RQ. *Who am I? What matters? What do I choose?*

We've witnessed this in the lives of many. Dave held both his professional ambition with his familial commitment and ultimately chose alignment over achievement. It was the Canadian doctor's invitation for Alice to hold the tension of what it meant to parent a toddler with Type 1 diabetes. A fierce mother, she held space for her son's new medical needs while grieving the life she thought he would have. Kate held the chaos of her workplace and found clarity to remain on a more grounded path.

When we are present, tension shows up everywhere: in our careers, relationships, and even our quiet moments of reckoning. We feel it internally in our commitments, values, relationships, and the choices we make. It's why fast, Shallow, and distracted can feel so compelling. When we slow down and release the need for control, let go of others' expectations, and turn inward, it can feel like a lot of tension. Yet when we do let go, we cultivate the stillness required to hold the tension and the wisdom it has to offer.

Tension is not something to be resolved but to be honored and held. My sister-in-law's wedding was a day filled with joy and loved ones. And yet, it was also one of deep sadness, as her beloved grandfather had died unexpectedly that very morning. It was a profound both/and—grief and celebration coexisting.

Both/and is always around us. Day turns into night. Music is both the notes and the silence. Life is a mix of highs and lows.

Too often, we accept unwritten rules such as that sadness overrides joy when it is both/and. We suppress joy around people whom we deem to be struggling. A friend captured this beautifully over Halloween. She was recently widowed unexpectedly and dressed as "Sadness" from the Disney movie *Inside Out 2*. She was hilarious and devastatingly accurate in the same moment.

As you live more Real, this chapter invites you to explore the role of tension in your own life, not as something to fix, but as something to feel. Because it is in the feeling that we begin to wake up, and refusing to feel can have dire consequences.

> **Ideas —> Action**
> Where do you feel the weight of tension?
> What feels most uncomfortable for you?

The Body Does Not Lie

Several years ago, I was negotiating a complicated real estate transaction with family members. For nearly ten months,

I held immense tension that felt deeply personal and all-consuming. I heard repeatedly that I *should* be able to hold it all, both what they wanted and what I wanted.

Time and again, I was told I *should* trust them, that they loved me, and that they knew best. Fatigued with what felt like two-against-one negotiations, I tuned out my inner wisdom.

I desperately wanted to believe that they, too, were holding what was best for all of us.

When an email thread was accidentally shared with me, my heart broke. The shock of discovering that they were reveling in what they believed was "having me over a barrel" was devastating. It was intense, gut-wrenching, soul-altering.

Only after we completed the transaction did I turn inward to recover. Then, I tuned into what my body had been trying to tell me. As I was lying down later that afternoon, I noticed what felt like dizzy spells—seven over an hour. Concerned, I scheduled an appointment with my primary care physician. A few tests later, it became apparent that my heart was literally broken. More specifically, I had a high-grade atrioventricular (AV) block, where one part of my heart could not consistently send energy to another part. This was the final physical sucker punch to what had felt like months of emotional beatings.

Although I was exceptionally fit, I'd ignored what my body had been trying to tell me. Now, in physical manifestation, it was showing me in the form of a heart rhythm disorder that could have killed me. While this is my story, I'm not alone. Ever wonder why athletes sometimes drop dead after a marathon? Despite their prowess, I am guessing that they, like me, missed (or ignored) physical signs that they'd pushed themselves too far for too long.

Most of us have our way of Shallowing and avoiding the tension. High achievers can be so focused on climbing the corporate ladder that they have no idea where it will lead or whether it or even ends up somewhere they want to be. But it gets worse. When we refuse to hold the tension and prioritize external objectives, it is all too easy to disconnect from ourselves, our relationships, and our own well-being. The result is that you and I gradually become numb to the needs of our own bodies, minds, and spirits. In other words, what we do not face can actually kill us.

The good news is that reconnection with our internal self is possible. Realing is the first step back from the brink of lost awareness.

- When we acknowledge how we disconnected from ourselves in the first place, we are in tension.

- We feel tension when we explore how we lost track of the voice inside us and what matters.
- When we tune inward and listen to our biological feedback and inner wisdom, we are in a state of tension.
- When we stop prioritizing external outcomes and validation alone, we are in tension.
- We are in tension when we start listening to our own truth, purpose, desires, and callings.

We open when we acknowledge our longing to be seen, heard, and valued. When we recognize who we are, we see ourselves distinct from our external accomplishments and other people's shoulds. (Hopefully, without needing a pacemaker as a reality check.) In its purest form, this work is the journey home. Realing helps individuals reclaim their identity, and to acknowledge they are *enough* and *worthy* of love.

Embrace Hard Things as a Gateway to Growth

During that phone call about my grandmother's death, my dad held the tension. In it, he illuminated the importance of feeling and even celebrating the full range of my emotions. Over the years, that experience and lesson became a ballast for me amid challenges. I'm drawn to people willing to be in tension, like I was drawn to the pregnant Holly at the fortieth birthday party.

Truisms exist for a reason. "What doesn't kill you makes you stronger" is one of them. "Adversity does not build character; it reveals character" is another. In our own lives, we each have the opportunity to be present and use hard things to create an existence we love, relationships we cherish, and a life without regrets.

Simple, right? Not at all. And becoming aware is a gateway to growth.

One of my mentors, Dr. Ann Marie Chiasson, consistently challenged me to broaden my lens of perspective and expand my perception of reality. She reminded me how we are conditioned to routinely judge others and pathologize problems. It's a pattern we believe will protect us when it Shallows our existence and truncates our capacity.

To counter that conditioning, she would ask, "What's right about that?" Considering situations through that lens opens our aperture of awareness to both/and. In contrast to finding the silver lining, this practice is an invitation into the Messy Middle. It's holding the tension of what is, all of it. And if we can be still with it all, often it becomes a clarifying recalibration about what truly matters. A profound opportunity to understand ourselves more fully and explore new mindsets that might better serve us in living Real.

While I don't seek adversity, I have learned to look at it differently. Like many couples, my husband and I struggled to start our family. The farther into infertility treatments we went, the more desperately I longed for kids. The more failed cycles, the more money we invested; the wider my drug-induced hormonal swings, the deeper I craved motherhood. And through all of it, I felt more pity from those around me.

So, what's right about that? I finally asked myself.

At the moment, it felt like nothing was right about it. But I can see with hindsight that our marriage deepened, we became more unified, and we were able to explore next-level interdependence. I was forced to navigate new depths of vulnerability and surrender. I've developed self-compassion, which has transformed me.

While we were blessed with a healthy outcome, kids bring challenges. When my son took off his diaper, fascinated by the massive poop and the opportunity to fingerpaint the walls, my mother reminded me, "You wanted this."

What's right about that? It wasn't hard to answer when I recalled the heartbreaking tenacity I'd mustered to help create that fabulous, fragrant, artistic mess of a human.

I'm not suggesting we be Pollyannaish or adopt an Instagram life approach to hard things. It's not about glossing over the hard to make them seem rosier. Instead, it's about opening to the full gamut of human experiences, both the awful and the amazing. When we can be in and with the tension, the more easily we learn, grow, and thrive.

It was by going through a season of grief, being fully and deeply emotionally in it, that I grasped the Shallowing of our lives. In holding my heartache, I could see others more fully. In that space, I felt our desperate collective desire to be, to feel more fully, and to live more Real.

I never intended to write another book, but at 4:03 a.m. on Sunday, December 8, 2024, I was awakened by an outline in my head for this book. My initial response, to myself, was to roll over, thinking, *No, thank you, two books, two kids, I'm done*. The tension persisted, and I listened enough.

Using grief as an opportunity for tension, the growth potential is immense. Research estimates that over two-thirds of the US population has been grieving the death of a loved one within the past two to three years. Deaths are a comfortable or societally recognized reason for grief, but there are endless reasons to grieve. Relevant data suggest that we are all experiencing difficult things and some type of grief. It might be loss of health, mobility, a job, a dream, or a role (such as parenting when kids leave for college). The end of a relationship or a divorce warrants grieving, too.

In reality, grief is a natural response to any kind of loss, not just a person's death. Holding the range of emotions, feeling the tension, and being with it is all you can do.

Though you can't usually change the situation, know it will transform you. Denying, dismissing, and stuffing emotions, as I learned with my heart, can have dire consequences. Realizing everybody around us is battling challenging situations and the feelings they elicit, usually some form of grief, can help prevent us from feeling like victims and make us more compassionate.

> **Ideas —> Action**
>
> Find three times to explore "What is right about this?"
>
> With this perspective, what else can you notice or see?

Sitting in Discomfort

Most of us have learned to avoid tension by distracting, fixing, or moving on quickly. We equate discomfort with danger. But in truth, discomfort is often the exact place where transformation begins because tension creates consciousness.

When you struggle with tension, notice the tightness you feel. That urge to escape the hard conversation, rush past the grief, and silence the deeper questions. Notice your impulse to turn away, change the channel, or bury yourself in email. That is the moment of growth. Not once is it resolved? Right there. In the middle of the mess.

A dear friend navigated a volatile marriage and was intimately familiar with post-fight tension. After a fight with her husband, regardless of whether it was a blow-up or a bicker, she would race to cover tension, desperate to feel better. *Was she afraid of divorce? Was she so dead set on being right that the possibility that she was in the wrong was too much?* When I invited her to explore a little deeper, why did she need things to feel better? She froze. Her need to simplify, distill, and reduce each fight to a black-and-white scenario was paralyzing her.

When we learn to sit in discomfort, we allow new insights or awareness to form. We allow ourselves to see what we have been running from—and why. That pause, that staying with, is what expands our capacity. It's what makes us wise. It's what allows insight to emerge from the inside out.

Realing is not about having it all figured out. It's about being honest enough to stay in the tension long enough to hear what your life is trying to say.

This is where growth happens. It is not in the resolution but in the willingness to feel. It is not in the fixing, but in the presence of a witness. It is not in bypassing discomfort, but in learning to be with it. It is in holding the tension of Realing.

My passion for Realing is palpable. It's not about saying you're doing something wrong; it's an invitation to see and be yourself fully. Acknowledge how hard it can be to pause and feel deeply in a world that asks us to speed up and move on. By allowing the full range of your emotions instead, you're investing in a much deeper, richer experience in life. Gaining that experience does not require an overhaul.

Micro-shifts can create the ripple effect needed for sustained change.

- Start small. Celebrate when you're aware and notice ways you stay present.
- Recognize ways you open more.
- Appreciate when you feel more.

Over time, the once unbearable discomfort becomes a welcome friend. A teacher. A mirror. A portal to more genuine, Real connections.

Realing might feel hard. And doing so can make forging more fulfilling relationships deceptively simpler. It means turning toward emotions rather than away from them. It means choosing presence over distraction. It means taking risks that feel vulnerable, rather than managing impressions.

Dr. John Gottman's research on relationship longevity identified "bids for connection"—those small moments when someone reaches for emotional engagement. In his findings, partners who "turned toward" these bids 86 percent of the time had relationships that thrived, while those who missed these moments had relationships that eventually failed.

These moments of turning towards one another are not grand gestures and are not limited to marriages. These are micro-decisions made countless times a day: putting down the phone when someone speaks, asking a question out of genuine curiosity rather than social obligation, listening deeply to feel what lies beneath the surface, sharing a struggle before it's neatly resolved, or simply acknowledging an emotion without rushing to fix it. We make these micro-decisions daily, every time we engage with ourselves and others.

When we can hold this level of presence for all interactions, we open a new layer of consciousness. We see how each small choice creates either connection or distance. We see how building these patterns compounds over time. Fostering RQ can create tension and help us to connect more deeply.

> ***Ideas —> Action***
>
> **What are small steps to begin?**
>
> **Where can you be more Real?**

When It All Feels Too Much

You are not alone. We all experience emotional overwhelm—those moments when it just feels like too much. In part because life has the full range, and in part because, in our Shallowing, our capacity to feel deeply and hold complexity has atrophied. Celebrate this awareness. It's when you can experience your overwhelm that you begin to Real. You're *feeling* something uncomfortable, instead of numbing it, and that, in itself, is a victory.

What are small shifts? While uncomfortable, *feeling too much* is a new opening. It gives us a glimpse inward. A chance to move toward ourselves, not away.

Remember the two widowed fathers: one who, after his toddlers were asleep, would set a timer for 20 minutes to allow himself to grieve; the other who scheduled acupuncture appointments simply to have a safe place to release what was bottled inside. These are examples of small shifts to open with presence.

Notice what draws you back to yourself. It could be stepping outside, breathing in the crisp air, and letting the sunlight warm your skin. Try writing what you feel or recording a voice memo to capture what's inside you.

Small actions give us a sense of direction and create space to be present. Engage a friend—"I've got a lot of emotions swirling, and I'm wondering if you might have time to connect. I would value your keen listening." We have forgotten the power of reaching out to a friend and how it can shift the outcome. Whatever you choose, start small, make small shifts, take steps forward, but just start.

Eight

Connect More Deeply

Living Real has the potential to transform relationships. Who knows your heart? Who trusts you with theirs?

At its core, Realing is not just about feeling emotions or healing heartache. It's about relearning how to be present and in relationships with ourselves, others, and the world around us. One of the most powerful outcomes of this work is the ability to rebuild relationships rooted in something more profound than convenience, performance, or routine. When we are Realing, we can cultivate honest relationships that are grounded, expansive, and nourishing.

These relationships start within.

We are being called, challenged, and sometimes forced to rethink what connection really means. The collective grief, isolation, and disruption we have experienced is a tension. For many, it exposes how fragile or surface-level some of our connections have become. For others, it sparks a deep longing: to be known, seen, and met with truth and presence. Living Real calls us to be more intentional in how we relate to one another, the spaces we gather in, and the energy we bring to our relationships.

Resistance Can Mask a Craving

Several years ago, I found myself seated under a sprawling Banyan tree at a dinner event next to a sharply dressed corporate litigator named Elizabeth. She was nearly twice my height, all edges and salt—intimidating, closed, and uninterested in small talk. Every attempt I made to genuinely connect was met with a verbal door slammed shut. Instead of withdrawing, I got curious. Who is she? What has she experienced that warrants this level of protection? Who is she below this polished exterior?

The dinner was structured around meaningful prompts that were shared while everyone sat around the table. Sitting just before Elizabeth in the rotation, I chose to be unapologetically Real—speaking with vulnerability, naming the power of presence, and modeling compassion. Slowly, something in Elizabeth began to soften.

By the night's end, long after the tables were cleared and other guests had gone, Elizabeth stayed rooted in her seat. It was as if she didn't want the evening to end because being seen—truly seen—was a foreign experience she didn't know she needed. Beneath her sarcasm and sharpness was someone tender, aching, and unfulfilled who longed to be connected.

I stayed behind. We talked. Elizabeth told me about her parents, loneliness, and the life that she had never quite chosen. And as we stood to leave, I felt both hope and heartbreak. Hope because she had let herself be known, and I played a role in it, and heartbreak because so many, like her, wear thick armor that can rarely be penetrated. Elizabeth reminded me that even the most guarded among us crave Real connection. Sometimes, we just need someone to stay long enough to open the door.

Overcoming the Connection Crisis

Elizabeth's story is just one thread in a much larger tapestry, the loneliness crisis referenced in Chapter 3, woven into our overconnected yet disconnected existence. That dinner showed me what I have witnessed repeatedly: human connection—Real, unfiltered, heart-felt connection—is the antidote.

I've listened deeply to leaders, visionaries, and seekers for two decades. The more present I am, the deeper I venture, the clearer it becomes. We are terrified of, yet starving for, something more Real.

To connect deeply, we have to show up fully. Not the polished, filtered version of ourselves, but the present, feeling, honest one. These kinds of connections can feel risky. It's no wonder many people flinch when someone speaks from the soul; it rattles their defenses. If you've already started Realing, you've likely felt others' resistance. It is not rejection; it's their discomfort with depth. Overcoming that discomfort begins within.

Vulnerability is not about oversharing or turning every meeting into a therapy session. It is about being comfortable with discomfort. It's about knowing the moments to lean in and be Real. It is about being still when the urge is to take action. It is about listening more deeply when the urge is to crack a joke. It is about being more present when the urge is to criticize, numb, disengage, or check out.

Realing invites others in. To calibrate on whether you are oversharing, ask these questions:

- Is there an interaction or an exchange?
- Are you filling the silence or monologing out of discomfort?
- Is there a shared interest in connecting more fully?
- Are others leaning in or out of this interaction? To the exchange

It is not about monologuing. It creates an interaction. It invites others to lean in, to feel.

Knowing how to Real is the gateway. It comes from within—from being honest with yourself first. Ask yourself: Where are you struggling? What are you avoiding? What part of you wants to be seen? That self-honesty becomes the doorway to genuine connection. When we lead with our humanity instead of our credentials, we invite others to do the same. And in a world desperate for depth, it's not just powerful, it's medicine.

We cannot offer others what we haven't first cultivated in ourselves. If we want a more authentic connection, we must begin by reconnecting to our truth. We open if we are present and hold the tension of our truths. When we build a solid inner foundation of self-awareness, self-trust, and self-compassion, we stop relating to performance, protection, or people-pleasing. Instead, we begin to live from a place of presence.

And when we are truly present, something shifts: We stop scanning conversations for the *right* response. We stop editing our truth to make others more comfortable. We stop hiding the messy parts of ourselves out of fear that they will not be accepted.

In that shift, we find greater depth. We open more. We find more tension, and we find even more depth. We see ourselves in a new light, with more compassion.

We begin to see our relationships differently. Conversations come alive. We start listening beyond words by feeling into tone, energy, and what's unsaid but profoundly true. We become less reactive and more responsive. We soften into curiosity instead of clinging to control. And we show up—not to impress, but to connect.

This is rebuilding our relationships, not from the outside but from the inside out. As we become more Real with ourselves, we permit others to do the same. That's the ripple effect of Realing. You become a space where depth is safe, where truth is welcomed. Where connection becomes a living, breathing thing again.

And that realization can change everything.

> ### Ideas —> Action
>
> What relationships need your attention?
>
> What needs more attention or space on your calendar?
>
> What is one action step you can take to support those who matter most?

Happiness Is Connection

One of the clearest truths about a good life is not glamorous or groundbreaking. It's simple. Quiet. Undeniable. The Harvard Study of Adult Development, the longest-running study on happiness, tracked lives for over eighty years. Its finding?

Fulfillment does not come from wealth, status, or even good genes. It comes from the quality of our relationships.

As Dr. Robert Waldinger put it: "Good relationships don't just protect our bodies; they protect our brains." Those most satisfied in their relationships at fifty were the healthiest at eighty. In a world chasing productivity and prestige, the Real sustainer is connection. Not followers or contacts. Real connections—the kind built on presence, not performance.

We have been conditioned to relate transactionally, so we manage impressions, stay likable but not too exposed. Here's the truth: Connection, which is the essential component of fulfillment, can't grow in that soil.

To move from performative to authentic, we do not need more effort. We need more courage. Courage to unlearn the belief that it is safer to be admired than to be seen. Remember that intimacy does not come from perfection but from presence.

- It starts with showing up as you are. Unguarded. In progress. Wholly in your humanity.
- It looks like asking the deeper question and holding space for the Real answer.
- It looks like telling the truth, even if your voice trembles.
- It looks like being with someone, not because they are useful, but because they are Real.

Vulnerability, Presence, and Realing

Part of Realing means being more intentional in forging Real relationships, like seeking out communities that value authenticity and welcome vulnerability. Support groups such as Alcoholics Anonymous have unifying practices to create community, foster genuine interaction, and forge deeper connections. Fitness classes attract people with shared values and create space for synchronicities.

We see how isolation can be as dangerous as smoking or obesity. We know the quality of our connections directly impacts our health, longevity, and overall well-being. We need relationships that are deep, genuine, messy, and present. This doesn't mean a day-to-day friendship or a 24/7 in-your-backyard friendship. These friendships don't always have to be close.

Forging genuine relationships is a practice, discipline, and investment. Ask yourself:

- Who would you trust your life with?
- Who do you turn to when you are at a crossroads?
- Where do you turn for candid feedback?
- Where are the spaces where you feel safe to be raw, vulnerable, and uncertain?

My dear friend, Dr. Victoria Maizes, calls these primal relationships; they are the connections so essential to us that they become like the air we breathe. Once experienced, they become vital and soul-nourishing. These are the relationships we collect over a lifetime of Realing. These are the people whom we know we can count on. While we all crave the depth of these connections, we often don't know how to form them.

Through my own journey of Realing, I feel rich beyond imagination in friendships. It is not about liking or clicking with everyone. I am certain that some, who are disinterested or unwilling to Real, will reject ideas in this book. It's about noticing when there is a spark and nurturing the connection. It's about knowing who feeds your soul and matters deeply to you and vice versa. Like my connection with Elizabeth under the Banyan tree, Real relationships are both a decision and a discipline.

I choose to be fed by my relationships, and I intentionally invest in nourishing these connections. I am blessed by female friends who have transformed my understanding of genuine connection. Their ethos, "go deep fast," is simple yet can feel revolutionary. We gather in beautiful, warm places with the expectation of unplugging from our busy lives, connecting with one another, and nourishing ourselves through learning and connection.

It can, without a doubt, be intense. Gathering passionate, driven, like-minded women can create immense energy. Being together, away from our lives, allows us to be even more present to one another and hold that complexity.

One evening, after a few margaritas, I casually asked someone new to the group, "So, what makes you tick?" By breakfast the next morning, she not only had not slept but appeared agitated and deeply uncertain. The tension sparked a deeper curiosity about what her passions were and whether she was living purposefully. At the right moment, a Real question changed her and her life's trajectory.

We might not need more friends. We need more Realness in our friendships. We might need more Tutu Tuba Parades. More opportunities for belly laughter. More sacred silence. More spaces where we can lay the mask down and just be. Because, in the end, it's not about who knows your name. It's about who knows your heart and who trusts you with theirs.

> ***Ideas —> Action***
>
> Forging genuine relationships becomes an intentional practice.
>
> Where can you be more clear on who and what matters?
>
> In what ways can you bring more Realness to your relationships?

Integrated Ideas into Action from Part II

You see the potential of both/and and are ready to shed what has been holding you back. With the right microshifts, you can hold more, be fully present, and rekindle energy.

To focus your energy, we've created quick, actionable tools to move from awareness into action.

Visit livingreal.AIMleadership.com/activities or scan this QR code to access reflection prompts and integration tools, or download our mobile app so you can stay connected to what matters most and engage support.

PART III

A GUIDE FOR LIVING REAL

As compelling and enlivening as it is to Real, it requires a new set of skills to be present in this full range of experiences, to hold the tension of both/and, and to interrupt old patterns. While it sounds compelling, living Real can be complex, confusing, and a lot.

In this final part of the book on integration, we will build on the mindsets for how to live more present to all of life—the messy and the beautiful, with strategies for how we can reconnect within ourselves (head, hearts, and body), for how we can hear and listen inward to our wisdom, for how we can be more present with the people we love, and ultimately, for how we can find more fulfillment going forward.

This section is designed as a toolkit for how to live more integrated, aligned, and present with fewer regrets.

I'll get more tactical in this section, offering guidance and structure, not as a rigid formula but as a starting place.

A scaffold. Something to try on, live with, and adapt. Be mindful of the urge to immediately change or adapt practices before trying them. What is being triggered within you by the practice? That instinct, while often well-intentioned, can sometimes be a subtle form of resistance—a way to avoid discomfort and growth.

Commit to exploring this part of the journey. Let it challenge you. Let it stretch you. Then, when the time is right, make it your own. Ultimately, this is about learning to hold space for yourself, so you can come home to what's Real.

> ### Ideas —> Action
>
> Where are you ready to stretch?
>
> What will you implement?
>
> How will you hold yourself accountable?

Nine

Build Our Inner Capacity

It's hard to paint a chair when you're sitting in it.

To stay present amid the complexity, we must build our capacity. With the right structures of support or containers, we expand our capacity to hold, process, and make meaning around hard things. A mindfulness practice might help you feel more grounded and centered. Exercise might help you release stress. A to-do list might help you feel organized. Each of these expands our capacity to stay present.

In my own journey, the most enduring, reliable capacity builders are internal. They come from deepening our understanding of who we are and what we need to be fully present. When we intentionally create structures, such as practices, habits, or mantras, we position ourselves to be our best selves.

Containers build our capacity to be Real. They provide structures that support our internal knowing, confidence, and sense of self. Containers or structures of support surround us and steady us from the inside out. Clarifying and strengthening these containers becomes a gateway to building our capacity to stay present.

Since this important concept is abstract, here's a metaphor. In a mother's womb, a baby is tightly contained and feels safe and secure. Being thrust into a new world can feel overstimulating, and a baby can cry inconsolably. Many new parents quickly master the swaddle—a blanket wrapped tightly, like a burrito, around a baby. Often, the screaming infant exhales deeply and becomes bucolically silent.

We need to understand our own swaddle, that container that will hold us and provide us with structure and security to venture bravely into this world.

Reclaiming The Path

Many of us find ourselves walking down a path in life that isn't what we had hoped or intended. When we can step back and get altitude, we gain perspective about what matters. We can intentionally understand where we are and what types of containers or structures we need to be set up for success.

Sam is a brilliant and driven woman who grew up in a large family and was accustomed to looking out for herself. Having lived around the world, working in different industries and various settings, she'd spent time reflecting on what was most important to her. Sam knew what she valued and had intentionally created a life she hoped would be good. She juggled a high-pressure, high-stakes role in a company she had founded. She felt little margin for error with other people's lives on the line.

When she found herself unexpectedly single parenting two young children, she questioned everything. There was grief in all of it—in parenting alone, in the isolation she'd never wanted but somehow created, in the shame of her marriage ending, in the abandonment and anger she couldn't shake.

One of the greatest gifts she gave herself and her kids was to take stock and feel it all. It was a lot and, at times, hard to hold. She felt the full range of those emotions. The depth of these feelings became a gateway to better understanding both what she truly wanted and what she needed to support her personally, professionally, and as a parent.

Thrilled to be a mother, she had never intended to do this alone, let alone without the support of loved ones. She was committed to creating a loving home that felt like a safe space, supporting her young children and ensuring they had opportunities to explore sports, music, and more.

Together, we distilled what mattered most to her: in her home, parenting, and work. With clarity on what she needed, we built a container to set her up for success. We designed systems to ensure she could put healthy meals on the table and have her children supported, first with childcare and then with transportation to and from activities. We worked to reduce degrees of freedom, knowing that the more we simplified things from holiday plans to meals to kids' clothes, the easier it would be to navigate all that was on her plate. We figured out how she would find ways to work out, build a supportive network of families in her community, and feel less alone on this parenting path.

Align with What Matters

If there's one invitation in all of this, it is to keep coming back to who and what matters.

It is so easy to get swept up in the noise—the urgency, expectations, and pressure to keep up. But most of the time, what drains us is not doing too much—it is doing too many of the wrong things. Things that are not aligned. That does not matter in the long run. That leaves us feeling empty instead of full.

Remember, you get to choose what matters to you. You get to realign.

When faced with a decision, ask yourself:

- Is this aligned with who I want to be?
- Am I spending my energy on what truly matters to me?

- Have I slipped into default mode—doing what's expected, not what's meaningful?

When we realign with what matters—our values, relationship, truth—life feels less like a grind and more like something we are living for.

You do not have to change everything overnight. But you can start by listening inward. Start by getting honest. Make small choices—daily ones—that move you closer to the life you want.

Living in alignment is not a one-time decision; it is a discipline, a returning, a remembering. And it is always available to you.

> ***Ideas —> Action***
>
> What is out of alignment for your life at this time?
>
> What do you need to shed to move forward?

Containers Build our Capacity

Imagine a playground that spans an entire city block. If the only boundaries are busy roads on all sides, with no transparent barrier to keep the children safe, the kids would naturally cluster in the middle, staying close to what feels more secure. But if the same playground is surrounded by strong fences that clearly separate the children and their play from the busy streets and traffic, the children can spread out easily. They could run freely, explore more fully, and use the entire space. The fence's structure does not limit their freedom; on the contrary, it creates it.

Just like this scenario, life without clear containers or structures often feels chaotic and overwhelming—this is why many of us retreat into Shallowness in the first place. We created "rules" about putting hard things into the metaphoric basement. Shallowing became a structure of support, albeit a short-sighted one.

It's through developing our capacity to set clear, supportive boundaries that we begin to hold difficult emotions, rather than bury them. Instead of shoving our feelings into the metaphorical basement, locking them away to deal with later or not at all, we create space to process them as they arise. We shift from emotional repression to emotional regulation.

We don't have to be consumed by our feelings, spilling them everywhere or broadcasting them online in a desperate scramble to make sense of them. Nor do we have to avoid them entirely. Instead, we can learn how to stay with what's hard, moment by moment, without running. We can learn to hold the tension, to walk through it, and in doing so, build the strength and self-trust to face whatever comes next.

Along this journey, you may have deepened your awareness by exploring and tracking what causes you to Shallow. You may have noticed where you resist being Real and what helps you to hold on to the complexity. The more that we know about ourselves, the more effectively we can craft containers that will expand our capacity to stay present.

Structures surround us. They come in the form of titles, roles, and responsibilities. They come in the form of rules, such as paying taxes and driving on the right side of the road. They come as agreements: If you loan me this money to buy a house, I will pay this monthly mortgage. We are surrounded by structures that contain us.

The challenge with Realing is that we often aren't intentional about crafting containers that nurture our capacity to be present and feel fully. The *right* containers help us be more present, process more complexity, and build awareness. And, just as it can be hard to paint a chair when you are sitting in it, we often struggle to see what we need. In Sam's case, as she moved through her emotions—anger, shame, exhaustion, and sadness—of single parenting, she could better see what she wanted. Sam intentionally created the structures she needed to feel supported in single parenting. With more awareness, she made small proactive decisions to hire help and invest in her local networks.

> *[DEF] Containers: Intentional structures that support our ability to be fully present, to feel deeply, to open into the best version of ourselves. Such boundaries or systems can be beliefs, practices, or tools that help us experience the full range of life, supporting us in our authentic connection with ourselves and with others.*

Intentionally crafting the right structures helps us hold and process hard things. Limiting the news one consumes is a way to stay present. Turning off technology at a particular time is a way to improve sleep. Exercising is a container for managing stress. At the core, we must understand what is essential and what we need to nurture. In doing so, notice beliefs, habits, and relationships that no longer support you and your desire to be present.

While I love my family, alone time is vital to maintaining my balance. I crave physical space to be still, reflect on my insides, and gain perspective. Much to my husband's chagrin, this is not just quiet time. Being physically alone makes me more present with my thoughts; I reflect on what matters, what is needed, and what is becoming. Family vacations are great and even better when I carve out alone time to be my best self.

My client, Sam, invited me to help rebuild her containers. She wanted to stay present and parent through all the complex, unexpected new things. Shedding any ego-driven desire, she detached from doing it *"right"* and committed to being the best parent she could be for her children.

We operate in a culture that is deafeningly loud. The outside world constantly tells us what we should think, feel, and believe. Clear containers are vital to being our best selves. With strong containers, we can stay present in the moment and not judge. They help us to adapt to changes and adjust to hold more. Strong containers are vital to listening inward, which we explore in the next chapter.

> *Ideas —> Action*
>
> What "containers" do you have in place?
>
> Where could you benefit from more structure?

Why We Resist Containers

For many of us, the idea of structure or containment brings up resistance. We've lived much of our lives within systems shaped by other people's expectations.

The inherited containers may have kept us functioning, but they often were not built for our flourishing. So, it's okay to ask: Do I really need this boundary? Is this rule mine—or someone else's? Can structure support me, or will it restrict me?

These are valid questions. And yet, the paradox is this: while we may resent or reject the rigidity of external systems, we often don't realize how desperately we long for internal ones—structures that help us feel safe, anchored, present, and free to inhabit our lives fully.

We also do not have to hold everything alone. As we begin to listen inward and identify our authentic needs, we can create containers and support systems that hold us, reflecting who we are, not who we have been told to be.

None of us would choose Sam's path, but there was something profound about her inner clarity, the way she allowed herself to be supported, and how clearly she stayed connected to her internal wisdom or metaphoric radio station. She was emotionally resilient. Within her intentional, well-built container, Sam thrived. It held her through loss and helped her remain connected with herself amid change.

Each of us can create containers like this in our own lives—structures that hold, support, and even nurture us. And we need them, not as cages or restrictions, but as frameworks that help us come home to ourselves.

With a supportive structure, we can feel more fully, with less fear and more grace. We can let emotions move through us instead of being overwhelmed or derailed. We can stay in relationship with ourselves, our loved ones, and what matters most. Structure is what allows presence. It will enable us to hold the tension without collapsing or shutting down.

Containers are the shapes we give to support our capacity to feel. The rituals, boundaries, habits, and rhythms help us stay connected to our inner voice when the noise outside gets loud. They help us navigate, not control, what life brings.

Realing is an invitation to rethink what matters by pausing and asking:

- What is essential?
- What does success mean to me?
- What does happiness look like beyond the formulas I've inherited?
- Which relationships enliven me? Which relationships activate me?
- What helps me embrace living more Real?

Shallowing offers an illusion that if you follow the script and stay positive, and if you achieve enough, you will feel successful. Realing does not promise that kind of control because it entails living with less certainty and more truth, less performance and more presence. It asks us to trade the black-and-white rules for the infinite shades of gray where Real life happens. It's not easy—but it's honest, and ultimately, it's what makes us more fully alive.

Be Clear on the Outcome, Flexible on the Approach

In her grief, Sam asked for help to make sure she retained her capacity to listen inward. We all have the capacity to be present, to listen inward, and to position ourselves for success as Sam did. While containers aim to bring structure into our lives, the concept itself is abstract and thus hard to grasp.

You have the capacity. These might be underused muscles that have atrophied. For so long, especially for women, we have been taught to take care of others and that listening inward to our own needs is selfish. At times, we feel shame for longing to hear that in inner channel that speaks wisdom. Every time we fly, during the safety briefing before departure, we are reminded of just how important it is to put on our own oxygen mask before trying to help those around us. And yet, in life, how rarely do we practice this?

The key is to start small and build awareness. Recall Chapter 6 and the two fathers who were widowed with young children. Clear that they needed space to feel, they each built safe containers. One scheduled 20 minutes to cry with reckless abandon, and the other booked twice weekly acupuncture session. They each started incrementally. They understood the need to be with sorrow and to keep living, parenting, and being.

Having the right structures in place provides a framework to regulate and modulate our emotional experiences, helping us determine what we can process in a given period without triggering fight-or-flight responses. Many parts of Realing are complex, can feel abstract, and at times like too much. Through structure, these fathers built their capacity to hold grief. This container makes it safer to navigate the more challenging aspects of life.

We first create this presence within ourselves, and it then extends to our relationships. When we have clarity about the outcome, we can then become flexible in our approach. We begin to metabolize grief and uncertainty rather than numb it away. This transforms fear from something that controls us into something we can move through.

Two Steps Forward, One Step Back

Once we see and understand Realing and Shallowing, it becomes almost impossible to unsee them. And sometimes being present with that becomes hard, in and of itself. We might engage with superficial fluff, knowing that we crave more genuine connections. Craving a Real connection can feel primal. It creates tension to see where we Shallow or have settled for Shallow relationships. Being present, observing, and taking ownership for our part is a massive win. It is the gateway to being at choice.

The goal is not to be 100% Real, 100% of the time. The goal is to take steps forward each day. To make microshifts towards being more Real. To be more true to who you are and who you were meant to be. To be more willing to listen inward. To be more able to hear and honor your own truth.

Carve out quiet spaces to reflect. Creating a consistent time, pattern, or habit helps.

- Where do you see Realing?
- Where can you be more Real? Why? What supports you?
- What is energizing about Realing? This is important and can become self-reinforcing.
- Where do you see Shallowing? Why? What is driving that?
- Where do you Shallow? Why? What triggers you to Shallow?
- What is depleting about Shallowing? Again, leveraging this for behavior change.

Our goal is more awareness, not judgment.

Explore small shifts that move you to more Real. It could be small, conversational shifts—being curious, inviting in-depth conversations, or listening below the surface. Chatting on the sidelines of our daughters' soccer game on a damp, cold morning, I asked another mom about a school event. She shared that she had missed it as she was visiting her parents. With a gentleness and presence, I probed a little deeper. "I honor how much time you invest in driving the six hours down to support them amid all that is on your plate…." Her emotional floodgates opened—her father had another ministroke, his care was more than her mother could manage, and they needed to make significant, hard decisions.

We all have emotional floodgates that are looking for release, looking to be cleared. The more presence we give to feeling, the less stagnation we experience. At first, releasing emotions can feel overwhelming, as if we are flooded and less in control. When possible, start small and in safer spaces. Consistency transforms raging rivers into trickling creeks.

Either emotions will be released or they will be repressed deep into your body, creating dis-ease. I am grateful for my bionic heart, and I wish that I had listened more deeply to my emotions. Sometimes feelings have been Shallowed for so long, they feel calcified and beyond reach. Another option is to explore ways to create space for others to release. While separated from your work, it still engages your emotions. Still hard? Find a movie that resonates with your feelings. Emotional tear-jerkers can be a great way to get emotions flowing.

How to Feel Again

Learning to feel again is not about getting swept away. It's about building the capacity to be with our emotions—present, grounded, and curious. It's the difference between being tossed in the storm and becoming the one who can sit at the edge of the waves, steady and awake.

Let me be clear: feeling is not always easy, pleasant, or something everyone wants to start with. But I sincerely believe this: You have within you the capacity to hold what you feel, building an internal oasis of stillness and strength, rooted in the truth that you are already good. Already whole. Already enough.

You do not need to fix yourself to begin feeling. You simply need to remember how to listen.

Here are some gentle ways to begin:

- **Create safety within yourself.**

    Notice the voice of your inner critic—the one that shames you for feeling too much or too little. Then soften. Speak to yourself the way you'd speak to a dear friend in pain. Your nervous system needs kindness more than critique.

- **Start small.**

  Resist the urge to dive into deep waters right away. Begin with manageable emotions. Notice mild frustration, quiet contentment, subtle disappointment. Build trust with yourself there.

- **Anchor in your body.**

  Feel inward. Tune into what is within your body. Is grief heavy in your chest? Is anxiety a tightening in your throat? Let your body be your compass. You do not need to name everything—just feel something.

- **Practice non-judgment.**

  Witness emotions as they arise. Allow them. They are not good or bad—they just are. Let them pass through you like weather across the sky. You do not need to control them.

- **Develop containment.**

  Reclaim choice. While you can notice all kinds of experiences, you do not have to feel into each of them. Pick one moment or one thought. Explore one more deeply.

Remember: Feeling is a skill, a remembering. Each time you turn toward your emotions with gentleness, you build the muscle of aliveness. This is the way to presence. To being here. With yourself. Fully. Again.

Ten

Learn to Listen Inwardly

Listen to the whisper that emanates from within.

We've spent so long listening to other people tell us who we should be, what we should do, how we should live, and what we should want that many of us have lost our ability to listen inwardly. With our new Realing mindset, we revisit what it means to listen more deeply.

Amid the deafening external barrage of shoulds, many of us struggle to hear, feel, or discern our inner wisdom. The right containers not only position you for success, but they also help you focus inward. This journey toward renewal begins with learning to listen inward and checking in on what you need in any particular moment. I recognize that these are abstract concepts and new skills that, while simple, are profoundly life-changing.

Layers of Listening

While we are always listening, we are seldom encouraged or even taught how to listen to ourselves inwardly. Yet, by turning our attention inward, we can unlock insights, intuition, and a greater sense of alignment. Building awareness allows us to hear in layers, recognize the filters that shape our perceptions, and discern what we hear, intuit, or disregard.

Listening, both externally and internally, is not just about sounds; it's about accessing deeper information and uncovering layers of understanding that might otherwise go unnoticed. Understanding these filters that we tune out, disregard, or ignore is a crucial step. By sharpening our ability to listen with intention, we can cultivate a richer, more nuanced awareness of ourselves and the world around us.

- **Close In:** Focus on immediate interactions and emotional dynamics.
- **Midway Out:** Observe community sentiments and broader dynamics.
- **Far Out:** Analyze the external trends and influences that shape your environment.

Listening is one of the five senses, yet it often weaves below the surface of our awareness.

Moving beyond "hearing," which is how we typically describe auditory stimuli, listening serves as a gateway to a deeper understanding and knowledge.

> **Ideas —> Action**
> How can you listen to hear the different layers?
> How might listening differently change your communication?

Shed the Shoulds

Life is not meant to be replayed over and over. I should have listened to my body. I should have trusted my intuition. Life is meant to be lived, fully present. Rather than continually replaying that transaction, I focused on metabolizing the feelings and growing forward.

We explored what it might mean to stop, let go, be still, listen inward, and be okay with not knowing. Now, we get to start living this, not as permission but as our truth. We get to listen inward to what enlivens us, to what fuels long-term feelings of happiness, fulfillment, and satisfaction.

We illuminated how tension creates consciousness. By learning to sit with discomfort and to hold tension, the next layer often reveals itself. For example, by observing and (hopefully) shedding the shoulds we have been carrying, we might open into new tensions or false beliefs such as

- I should be farther along.
- I should be more grateful.
- I should work harder.
- I should be over this by now.

Examining new layers is a vital part of Realing. These quiet, critical scripts often shape our choices more than we realize. They create pressure without clarity. They direct performance without alignment. I love the truism, "A horse designed by committee is a camel." A life designed by shoulds might look "successful" from the outside but feel hollow on the inside.

The truth is that most *shoulds* belong to someone else. They are inherited values, conditioned beliefs, or assumed commitments. They rarely lead us to a deeper, more aligned, and enlivened way of being.

Shedding is not about rejecting structure or responsibility. It is about pausing long enough to ask:

- What happened? What was my role in this? What can I learn moving forward?

- Which of these values, beliefs, and commitments align with what matters to me?
- When I am deeply present, what is rooted in truth, or in fear?
- Where am I living out of obligation? How can I live from intention?

Shedding the *shoulds* creates tension. It requires honesty. It asks us to untangle our identities from our roles. It beckons us to stop confusing being busy and being purposeful. It invites us to see worth as something we choose rather than something to earn through exhaustion or approval. Something powerful opens when we make space for what we want, value, and for who we are as opposed to who we have been told to be.

This work requires honesty.

Shedding *shoulds* is not rebellion. It is deliberately returning and choosing a life that's rooted in what matters to you.

- You don't have to follow the expectations others have for you.
- You do not have to apologize for evolving.
- You are allowed to let go.

This is where Freedom begins.

Let Go of What No Longer Serves

There comes a point in our growth when holding on costs more than letting go. By uncovering other people's truths that we had accepted as facts, we let go of old patterns, roles, or identities. These illusions once protected you, shaped you, and maybe even got you here. But that does not mean they belong in the next chapter of your life.

There is wisdom in letting go. It is not failure, but rather clarity. It is a choice to stop dragging what no longer fits you and to start walking lighter, freer, and more aligned.

Ask yourself these questions:

- What am I still carrying out of habit, not intention?
- What expectations or beliefs no longer serve who I'm becoming?
- What stories am I telling myself that keep me small, stuck, or safe?

This process is not always clean or comfortable. Letting go can feel disorienting, especially when you've built parts of your identity around what you are now releasing. But purpose evolves. And sometimes, the bravest act you can do is loosen your grip on something that once made sense but no longer does.

You are not obligated to stay the same. What served a purpose in one season or stage of life may be the very thing that is holding you back at this moment. Let it go with gratitude. Rather than resenting what you are releasing, bless it and move forward.

Letting go is not about loss; it's about making space for what is next, what is true for you now, for the version of you that has been waiting for permission to rise.

That permission starts here and now.

Practice Listening Inward

- Take a breath.
- Soften your gaze, or even close your eyes for a moment.
- Now ask yourself: *When was the last time I truly listened inward? When was the last time I trusted my inner knowing?*

Not to your calendar. Not to your inbox. Not to someone else's expectations. But to you. To the quiet knowing beneath the noise. For many of us, that kind of listening feels unfamiliar—even uncomfortable. The truth is, this act of tuning in with gentleness, grace, and compassion has become a forgotten practice, an atrophied muscle in a world that has trained us to look outward for answers. Yet it is through this very practice that we begin to reconnect with ourselves. It's here that healing begins.

You may notice some resistance. That's okay. It is expected. Listening inward often stirs up fear, not because we are broken, but because, deep down, we know that once we hear the truth, we can't unhear it. And with truth comes choice.

You've likely seen how we try to avoid this. We often make light of midlife crises, buying shiny cars, and filling our schedules. We keep moving fast enough to avoid the stillness. It's easier, sometimes, to let the ego take the wheel as it whispers, "You are fine. Just keep going."

But what if you paused long enough to listen? What might you hear? There's a voice inside you that is steady and wise. A cadence that's uniquely yours. A deeper current of knowing that's been there all along, waiting—not to shout over the world, but to speak with clarity once you quiet the noise.

This is not about getting it perfect. It's about slowing down, making space, and letting the practice be simple. It allows it to be enough to listen inward, to honor the whole spectrum, and not to take the convenient or socially acceptable path. This work is deeply personal. It is often uncomfortable. It can be profoundly freeing.

You may not have done this before. Celebrate the first step. Most of us are beginners in Realing. We live in a world that is loud, fast, and built for distraction. Listening inward can feel unnatural at first. It asks us to turn down the volume of the external world and begin asking unfamiliar but essential questions like these:

- Who am I?
- What matters most to me—not to others?
- What do I need to be the best version of myself, not in theory, but in this moment?

This is not always easy work. But it is honest. And it is how we begin the process of coming home to ourselves.

> ***Ideas —> Action***
>
> Take time to review the questions throughout this chapter. What have you started to notice within you?

Eleven

Engage Depth

We can open from presence when we have a solid inner foundation of self-awareness, self-trust, and self-compassion.

We live in a world that rewards the surface, such as being efficient, likeable, "fine." But beneath the surface, so many of us are carrying a quiet ache. The ache of being unseen—even by ourselves. Disconnected from our truth, we have drifted away from what matters most. This is why creating space for Realness within and between us is not just meaningful work, but is foundational.

It starts inside. You cannot offer presence to others if you are exiled from your own. You cannot hold space for someone else's truth if you are not in a relationship with your own. When you create space to feel what you feel, name what you need, and witness yourself without judgment, you begin to return to your center. That reconnection—small, steady, sacred—is the root of everything.

Ask yourself these questions:

- What part of me have I overlooked or been rushing past?
- What truth am I avoiding?
- What would it mean to be on my own side today?

Pause and consider your responses. As you listen inward, start to notice:

- Can I listen? Can I feel what is arising?
- Can I soften my urgency to fill the silence and just let it breathe?
- When I'm still, what do I need right now?
- How can I resist my urge to take action, help, or fix?

When you can meet yourself with compassion, presence, and honesty, something shifts. You stop abandoning yourself in subtle ways. You soften. You become less reactive and more responsive. And from that grounded place, you create space for others, not as a performance, but as an extension of your wholeness. We are accustomed to giving to others what we most crave for ourselves.

Being present with others does not require grand gestures. It can begin the moment you pause before responding. In this way, you ask a deeper question and stay long enough to hear the answer truly. In your willingness to sit with discomfort rather than bypass it. To say: "You don't have to be okay right now. I'm not here to fix you. I'm here to be with you."

This is how we disrupt the performance culture that keeps us lonely. This is how we replace transactions with transformation. We don't need more perfectly curated connections. We need the kind that lets us show up messy, human, and whole.

The truth is that space for Realness is medicine. It heals what disconnection has fractured. It quiets the noise. It brings us home to ourselves and each other. And from that place, we begin to live, not just exist together.

Realing Is a Choice

Not everyone is interested or ready to Real. Emotional intelligence is vital to read situations. Sometimes people need to warm up and reconnect before opening up emotionally. Just like that mom on the soccer field whose father was not well, sometimes we need an invitation to share.

One evening, as I tried to get in my steps, I was walking around my son's lacrosse field when another mom joined me. It was great to catch up as she shared about their travel, kids' sports, and more. I leaned in to share more about how this year felt easier, as she knew about my uncles' deaths last year, but was buffered by the intensity of writing this book. Leaning in more deeply, she shared the complexity of their winter, including the death of her father-in-law and how relieved she was that his service was over and now they were moving into logistics.

I felt a warm glow as she seemed to exhale into our conversation. It was the gift of relaxing, exercising, and spending time with a friend.

And, almost like a metronome, she would pivot the conversation back to me as if pre-programmed for finite self-disclosure. I welcomed her question and also acknowledged just how much I appreciated hearing what she was navigating. And so she continued.

At the end of the conversation, she said, "Thank you. There are times when I default to and enjoy light, fluff conversations like talking about cute sneaker trends and such. But wow, this was great. I didn't realize how much weight I had been carrying."

Spotting Shallowed Relationships

Not every relationship is meant to last forever. And not every relationship that has drifted needs to end. Some just need to be rekindled, and others may need to be lovingly released.

To know which is which, we need to get honest about where things stand.

Start by noticing the feel of the connection.

- Does it energize or drain you?
- Do you feel safe being Real—or do you find yourself shrinking, performing, or going through the motions?
- Has it become surface-only, polite but hollow? A Shallowed relationship does not always mean it is broken—it just means the depth is missing. If there is safety and energy, it can be repaired.

And, sometimes, that's because the relationship has run its course. There are people who enter our lives for a reason: to teach us something, shift us, and wake us up. Others come for a season, a chapter of life we shared but no longer live in. Some are meant for a lifetime, but even those can be Shallow when unspoken hurt, distance, or distraction wedges its way in.

Shallowed + Done

If a relationship leaves you feeling chronically unseen, disrespected, or diminished, despite efforts to reconnect, it may be time to release it. This is not about blame. It's about truth. Ask yourself:

- Am I holding on out of guilt, habit, or fear?

- Do I feel more like myself or less when I'm around this person?
- Have I tried to revive the connection and been met with indifference or resistance?

Letting go does not mean the love was not Real. It means you are honoring that its role in your story may be complete. Release with grace. Bless the past. Free up space for what's Real now.

Shallowed + Rekindling

Some relationships have simply gone dormant. Life got busy. The pain went unspoken. You both pulled away slowly. But something in you still cares and still wonders. These relationships can be revived, but only if you are willing to initiate with vulnerability.

Ask yourself:

- Is there unresolved hurt that needs to be named?
- What would it look like to go first—to share honestly, without expectation?
- Can I invite depth back in, even if it feels awkward at first?

Try this: Reach out with a voice note or message that says, "Hey, I've been thinking about you. I miss how we used to connect. If you are open, I'd love to catch up, hear how you are, and to Real—and yes, I am happy to explain." Small, brave gestures can spark surprising reconnections.

The key is discernment. Some people are worth leaning into again. For others, it's okay to bless and let it be. Either way, you reclaim your energy when you stop tolerating the Shallow for the sake of history. And you begin to build relationships—new or renewed—that are rooted in what's Real.

> ***Ideas —> Action***
> Review your relationships.
> Which relationships are Real vs Shallowed?
> What changes do you want to make?

When You Shallow

Be gentle. Acknowledge what happened and celebrate the fact you noticed. When possible, explore the patterns that might have contributed. What was challenging or uncomfortable? What is it you want? Reconnecting to who you are and how you want to be is vital. Whether you are

Realing or Shallowing, each has the potential to be a learning moment. Take the learning.

Here are a few personal examples. I know that I Shallow by drinking alcohol. It numbs my sensitivity and helps me feel more comfortable. If you are unsure how you Shallow, ask your partner or dear friends. My friend, the guy from the Tutu Tuba Parade, is a great mirror. "When you are less comfortable in a setting, you overfunction. You overtalk, and when it's really bad, you name-drop. It is as if you want others to recognize you as someone important or valuable enough to care about." Yes, his comments landed with a zing. When I softened and opened up to what was beneath my feelings, he was not wrong.

We all Shallow. The goal is to increase our awareness and be more at choice. This is the essence of Real Intelligence. It is a muscle that can be built over time with practice and presence. Shallowing happens all around us; we have been conditioned and patterned to avoid discomfort, numb, and stay safe. Realing is a new muscle that can feel like hard work. Be gentle.

Rebuilding Through Vulnerability

Vulnerability is not about oversharing. It is about investing in the connection. It is what happens when we stop trying to manage how we are seen and allow ourselves to be. It is what arises when we let presence replace protection—when we choose to be with what is alive in us without armoring or editing.

Vulnerability invites intimacy. When we speak from the unarmored places, when we share not just the story of our pain but the heartbeat within it, we create the conditions for deeper connection. The kind that does not demand we be more than we are. Just that we be here.

Twelve

CREATE SPACE FOR PRESENCE

Presence is our most precious asset. Embracing, nurturing, and sharing our presence with those we love is our most precious gift.

Thank you. We've come a long way together. Not in miles or metrics—but in awareness, in honesty, in your willingness to sit with what is hard, what is Real, and what has been waiting underneath the noise. If you are reading this, it's because you've already started to see more clearly. You've recognized where you've been performing instead of participating, surviving instead of inhabiting, skimming instead of sinking in.

So now, the question is not what else you need to learn. The question is, what needs to shift so that you can live what you already know?

You know the cost of Shallowing. You've tasted the clarity of slowing down. You've felt the ache of disconnection and the pull toward depth. You've begun to unlearn the lies: That more is better. That busyness is a sign of value. That worth is correlated with success, money, or fame.

And you've started to sense the truth: That presence is the soil where meaning grows. That aliveness lives in the full wave. That connection begins when you stop trying to be good and start choosing to be Real.

This chapter is where knowing becomes embodiment, where concepts become commitments. Where you stop trying to fit presence in—and, instead, make space for it to lead. So, how do we create more space to be fully present?

Slow Down and Time Bends

Time is not something we find—it's something we create. It's not about adding more hours, but about changing how we use the ones we have.

I remember sitting with Elena on her back porch, the evening light filtering through autumn leaves. She'd spent years chasing the mirage of "more time"—productivity hacks, efficiency systems, endless to-do lists that somehow never got shorter.

"I am always running," she said, watching a cardinal land on her bird feeder. "Always behind."

The irony was not lost on either of us. How could Elena simultaneously be in constant motion yet feel stuck in place? Holding that tension illuminated what many of us miss: the problem is not time itself, but our relationship with it.

Her truth came not through a productivity breakthrough but through a personal hardship. She was faced with her mother's unexpected diagnosis, which forced her to step away from all that she knew as routine. And in the slow, sacred days of caring for someone she loved, Elena discovered something surprising: When she was fully present—not half here, half somewhere else—she felt time take on a different texture altogether.

"Those weeks contained everything," she told me later. "They were both the longest and shortest of my life."

This paradox lies at the heart of our struggle to be more present. When we rush through moments, perpetually focused on what's next, we create a strange time warp: days that vanish without a trace, weeks that blur together, and years that somehow both pass slowly and fly by. My mentor, Dr. Ann Marie Chiasson, says, "Slow down and time bends."

There are moments when we are creating something meaningful, lost in conversation with someone we love, or simply awake to the texture of our own existence, where time is no longer linear but instead bends. The clock does not govern these moments. They open into something more vast.

I've come to believe that we don't actually want more time. We want more aliveness. We want more presence within time.

This is not about grand productivity philosophies or the morning routines of billionaires. It's much simpler and more profound. It begins with noticing where your attention goes when you are not directing it. What are you avoiding when you reach for a distraction? What happens when you allow yourself to feel what is present instead of rushing past it?

Recall the pathway to Realing:

R—Remove what is misaligned, distracting, or no longer serving.

E—Engage more deeply.

A—Allow the full range of feelings.

L—Let yourself be even more fully present.

> **Ideas —> Action**
>
> How can you create more space for what matters?
> How can you make this practice of living
> Real your own?

Welcome More Presence

Once we have recognized how we have been living in the Shallow, we can explore what it means to be more present, to experience the full spectrum of our experience, and to embrace both the depths and the heights, the shadows and the light.

The questions we ask shape the lives we lead. The prompts that follow will invite you to get more Real with yourself, to hold the tension, and open the doorway for your even deeper presence. Each is an invitation to pause, to feel, and to listen for what is true. Some may resonate immediately; others might feel uncomfortable. Discomfort itself is information that may signal where growth awaits.

Take these slowly. Permit yourself to be honest. The point is not to find perfect answers but to create space for your wisdom to emerge. This practice is not about adding more to your life—it's about removing the layers that separate you from what is already there, waiting to be felt.

Embrace Realing

Life is not a steady state of happiness—it's a sine wave of experiences, constantly moving through peaks and valleys. When we trust this rhythm instead of fighting it, something shifts. The lows become passages rather than prisons, and the highs become more vivid and more embodied.

Learning happens in the full range, with questions like these as your tools:

- What messages have I internalized about "staying positive" or "looking on the bright side"? How have those beliefs limited my emotional range?
- What am I afraid might happen if I allowed myself to fully feel my lowest moments?
- How might honoring my valleys—not rushing through them—expand my capacity for genuine joy?

Realing becomes a way of being that is captivating and enlivening. With practice, it creates self-renewing energy.

Feel Fully

Name hard things. Recognize the urge to numb yourself. Invite feelings as a teacher.

- In what areas of my life have I gone comfortably numb—and what might that numbness be protecting me from?
- What emotions have I learned to push away or hide? How would it feel to welcome them back as teachers?
- If I could speak honestly about my grief, without rushing to silver linings or minimizing feelings, what would I need to say?

This is the deeper work of being human. Resist the urge to override or minimize emotion. Instead, open with curiosity and courage. That which we are unwilling to feel will repeat.

Seek Enlivenment

Truth and courage align. Lies, illusions, and old beliefs fall away. New possibilities emerge.

- When was the last time I felt fully, unapologetically myself? What circumstances allowed that authenticity to emerge?
- What truth am I finally ready to acknowledge—even if only to myself?
- What small step can I take today toward living more authentically, more in alignment with my inner knowing?

Remember: Realing is a wild ride of authenticity—it is the undoing of performance altogether. It's when we stop trying to be seen in a certain way and instead allow ourselves to be experienced for who we are.

Recognize Shallowing

We begin by seeing more clearly where we have disconnected, denied, checked out, or numbed. We see that we've traded depth for safety and authenticity for approval. By illuminating the patterns that have kept us skimming the surface of our lives, we open ourselves to new possibilities.

Expose the illusion of success and perfection. Make space for the uncurated self.

- Where am I not engaging in my life?
- What parts of me have I sacrificed to maintain that image?
- When did I first learn that being "fine" was safer than being honest? What truth am I most longing to express but haven't—and what would happen if I finally gave it voice?

As short-term alluring as it is, Shallowing drives disconnection. Loneliness, burnout, anxiety, and depression are the stacked costs of generational disengagement.

The House Metaphor

Refuse to stuff hard things in the basement. Minimizing feelings does not make them go away or get easier. It denies us joy and growth.

- Where am I keeping things out of sight, out of mind?
- Why am I avoiding these experiences? Which one needs my attention the most?

- What would it feel like to reclaim a part of myself?

Embracing hard things takes courage and compassion. Start small. Build presence. Commit to connecting with your whole self.

Beware of Activation

Tune into the lure and cost of adrenaline. Urgency, stress, and cortisol drive exhaustion. Activation detaches us from what matters.

- Where in my life am I running on adrenaline and feeling a sense of urgency?
- Where might I invite more alignment, a more grounded presence?
- Am I comfortable in moments of stillness? When I slow down, what begins to surface?
- What might it feel like to build a life powered by energy that nourishes me rather than depletes me?

As captivating and focusing as stress can be, there are often hidden, unintended consequences. Microshifts can align purpose with outcomes, creating a more energized momentum.

Engage Growth

Be aware and integrate. Aliveness happens in the highs and lows. Shift from surviving to inhabiting.

- What qualities would characterize a life that feels deeply mine, not impressive, not perfect, but Real?
- Where am I still hesitating to choose my own becoming? What's at stake in that hesitation?
- What one small step am I ready to take this week that would bring me closer to my own aliveness?

Step into living more Real with compassion. Recognize that this is a new skill set that brings new ways of being open and vulnerable. Pace your opening, stick with it, and celebrate the small wins.

Both/And

Life is complex and filled with shades of gray. Seeing lows is not the same as seeing highs. Feeling good is not denying bad

- What are the costs or resistance to holding both?
- How might I simplify or Shallow?
- Where can the complexity of both/and build awareness or presence?

- What wisdom is inside the both/and versus the either/or of this current situation? How can I lean into my inner knowing?

There is grace in accepting uncertainty and letting go of the need to know. When we hold both, even when they conflict, we open up to a fuller and multidimensional way of being.

The Messy Middle

Embrace the space in between. Settle into uncertainty. Chaos is part of becoming.

- What part of my life or identity is currently shedding or transforming? What am I afraid to let go of in this process?
- Where am I waiting for perfect clarity before taking action? What might happen if I moved forward anyway, bringing my questions with me?
- What if this very discomfort, this uncertainty or transition, is not something to rush through but an essential part of my becoming?

Transformation rarely feels clean or comfortable. It is messy, disorienting, and often looks nothing like we expected.

But this middle space—what anthropologists call "liminal space"—is where the most profound growth happens.

Individuation and Identity

Reclaim the self beneath conditioning. Rewrite what "a good life" means.

- What inherited values or beliefs am I carrying that no longer feel authentic to who I am?
- Where have I abandoned my knowing or intuition to belong or be accepted?
- Who am I becoming when I stop trying to be who I was told to be?

We are journeying toward becoming more fully ourselves. Bringing gentle curiosity to what we were told creates space to understand what we truly believe. Seeing who we are opens the possibility of who we want to become.

Emotional Range + Integration

Feeling as access to wisdom. Tension is the doorway.

- Which emotion do I judge most harshly in myself? What wisdom might that very emotion be trying to offer me?

- What would it look like to follow a feeling all the way through—not to fix or change it, but simply to experience it completely?
- What has my body been holding or knowing that my conscious mind hasn't yet acknowledged?

Our emotions are not problems to solve—they are intelligence trying to reach us. When we listen to them rather than judge them, they become teachers rather than disrupters.

Hold Tension to Open

Find stillness in chaos. Be present in uncertainty. Build awareness.

- When I am still, where do I feel discomfort?
- Where and how do I avoid tension or discomfort?
- What am I trying to resolve quickly by getting out of this discomfort?

Tension creates consciousness when we are willing to stand in that space of discomfort. Our emotions are not problems to solve—they are intelligence trying to reach us. When we listen to them rather than judge them, they become teachers rather than disrupters.

Invest in Relationships

Build relationships that are rooted in presence, truth, and depth.

- With whom have I created distance, not out of malice but self-protection? What might be possible if I bridged that gap?
- What conversation am I avoiding that, if approached with honesty, might set me free?
- How might my relationships transform if I focus less on managing impressions and more on showing up honestly?

Commit to how you want to show up for and nourish the relationships in your life. Most people crave genuine connection. Explore how you can be more present, see them more fully, and understand what they are saying and feeling. Share of yourself, both in your presence and vulnerability.

Live with Depth

Illuminating old patterns and intentionally investing is a practice in building depth. Understand what you need to embody this deeper way of being.

Invest in Containers

Structures are supported. Boundaries are a practice. Feel without judgment.

- What practice or structure helps me feel safe enough to be honest with myself?
- What relationships, spaces, or rituals allow me to be unmasked and still feel secure?
- Where do I need to create a new container in my life to safely face what I have been avoiding?

Containers are not constraints—they are protection for what matters most. Like riverbanks that do not restrict the water but give it direction and power, good containers do not limit your emotional life; they make it possible to flow at full strength without flooding or dissipating.

Listen Inward

Find the stillness beneath the noise. The voice that does not shout but knows.

- What truth have I heard in my quietest moments that I haven't yet acted on or acknowledged?
- How does my body communicate wisdom that my mind dismisses or rationalizes?

- What would it mean to become someone I trust again—to honor my knowing?

The loudest voice is rarely the wisest one. Learning to listen beneath the noise of shoulds, other people's expectations, and cultural messaging is a practice that becomes more refined over time. Start by simply noticing the difference between thoughts that tighten your body and thoughts that allow it to soften and expand.

Connect Inward

See yourself fully. Recognize courage and willingness to grow. Be present.

- How can I build the connection within myself?
- How do I know when I am disconnected from myself? What patterns or behaviors show up?
- What aspects of myself have I silenced? How can I begin to listen inward to this voice?

Great relationships with others grow out of great relationships with ourselves. Opening more fully inward can feel uncomfortable. The presence of this tension opens us to more of who we are and how we are meant to be.

Connect with Others

See one another fully. Value who they are. Be present.

- In conversations, how do I truly listen to someone without needing to fix, advise, or respond?
- What guards or walls have I built around connecting with others?
- What would it feel like to be more open in my interactions?

Relationships are foundational. Connecting even more deeply with another, we open into more of who we are and how we are meant to be. Connection is an invitation to infinite possibilities. Lean in.

Build Vulnerability

The shift from control to connection. From certainty to possibility. From performance to presence.

- What do I believe vulnerability means? How has this shaped my ability to be vulnerable?
- Where might I be choosing safety over connection, pulling back, editing, or performing instead of showing up fully?
- What areas am I afraid others will see if I open up?

- What are the costs of not allowing myself to be vulnerable? In life, relationships, and leadership?

Being fully present requires a surrender. Letting go of what we think, stepping into the tension. In these new, vulnerable places, we open again.

Invest in Presence

Slow down, and time bends. Share your greatest gifts with those who matter most.

- Where am I choosing distance or control instead of intimacy and vulnerability, and what am I protecting through that choice?
- What feels most challenging about being fully present with others? With myself?
- How would my relationships change if I stopped trying to be impressive and focused on being available instead?

In pursuit of more, we have become enslaved by efficiency, productivity, and impact. Quality trumps quantity. Full presence creates a depth of time.

Presence in Real Time

Catching yourself Shallowing creates the opportunity to pivot toward greater presence.

1. **Pause:** Even a momentary delay can interrupt automatic patterns. Take a breath. Sip water. Feel your feet on the ground. This creates a space between the stimulus and the response.

2. **Name it:** Silently or aloud, simply acknowledge what's happening: "I notice I'm disconnecting right now" or "I can feel myself going into performance mode." Naming creates altitude and perspective.

3. **Get curious:** Ask yourself with genuine interest: "What am I trying to protect here? What would being fully present require of me in this moment?"

4. **Choose:** Make a conscious decision on how you want to proceed. Move not from habit or comfort, but from your deeper values and intentions.

5. **Take one small step:** Move toward authenticity in a manageable way. Perhaps share something more vulnerable, ask a question you want the answer to, or stay present for a moment longer than feels comfortable.

Remember that the goal is not perfection. It's about developing the awareness to notice when you've drifted and the capacity to return, again and again, to what's truly Real.

When we embrace our capacity to be present, we inevitably encounter tension—cognitive dissonance between who we are and how we are living, or between what we value and what we choose. This tension is not a problem to solve. It is energy that can fuel transformation.

As you work with these practices, you will begin to experience shifts—subtle at first, then more profound. You might notice these feelings:

- A deepening sense of connection with yourself and others
- More space for what truly matters
- A shift from reactivity to intention
- A growing capacity to be with difficulty without being overcome by it
- A remembering of who you are beneath the noise

This is the beginning of coming alive to yourself—not as a distant goal, but as a present possibility, available in each moment you choose to return.

> ### Ideas —> Action
> Deepen your experience. What resonated most?
> Where did you connect deeper to your life,
> your relationships, your Realness?

Live Real with Greater Ease and Impact from Part III

Thank you for investing in your capacity to Real. You see the power and possibility when we listen inward, engage with greater depth, and create more space for more presence.

Microshifts root us amid change and integrate what's resonating. The practical tools are designed to activate clarity amid complexity—simple prompts, short practices, and space to reflect.

Visit livingreal.AIMleadership.com/activities or scan this QR code to access reflection prompts and integration tools, or download our mobile app so you can stay connected to what matters most and engage support.

Conclusion

Coming Alive

One breath. One moment. One step.
All we have is here, now.

I hope that this book has helped you come closer to yourself. That in some way, big or small, it has brought you into greater awareness of what it means to truly feel, to be present, to become alive to your own life again. Not just surviving it. Not just checking the boxes. But showing up—showing up—for the one life you get to live.

If there's been a thread through all of this, it is this truth: We've been wanting more. Not more stuff, more success, or more busyness, but more depth, more meaning, more connection. We've been wanting a life that feels like our own.

We do not get there by avoiding the hard things. We get there by facing them. Feeling them and moving through them. That's where our aliveness is waiting, not in the easy, but in the honest.

And I hope, through reading this book, you've seen how that shift is possible. How becoming more present, more Real, more you is not some lofty goal. It is a process. One that starts with awareness, with courage, and with the decision to stop running from yourself.

The world is changing. Fast. We are in tough times—politically, socially, economically, in a world full of loneliness, burnout, depression, and anxiety. We are suffering at the individual, family, and community levels. And there are so many feelings that we don't know how to feel, process, metabolize, or release. We have defaulted to repressing and dismissing these struggles, and it is only making these situations more difficult.

During the writing of this book, the world has been grieving on a global level. We live in a time when we are forced to review all aspects of life at a rapid rate, including wide-ranging changes in employment, societal norms, and programs that have historically brought safety and a voice to the unheard. We desperately need something to anchor us, which means taking an honest look at how Shallow our experiences have become. We must get Real with one another. We can no longer afford to live an Instagram life. We need to become comfortable with the tension of the uncomfortable and use it to embrace a fuller, more empowering life.

While the concepts in this book apply to many groups—families, teams, and communities, I hope you will embrace living Real in a personal way that will allow you the presence, energy, and capacity to serve those around you. Just as we are reminded to put on our oxygen mask before helping others, living Real yourself will give you the reserve you need to help someone else.

We don't have forever to keep putting off the life we're meant to live. We have to choose it.

So, if there's one thing I hope you walk away with, it's this: You are not behind. You are not broken. You are not too late. Now is the time to start Living Real.

FURTHER READING & BONUS RESOURCES

*L*iving Real doesn't end here. In many ways, this is where the Real journey begins.

We've created a set of additional resources to help you continue this work in your way, at your own pace. These supplemental resources are intended to support you in staying present, going deeper, and integrating what you've begun to awaken in yourself.

Visit livingreal.AIMleadership.com/activities or scan this QR code.

Acknowledgements

More often than I care to admit, I have resisted listening inwards. Sometimes I haven't wanted to hear all that is beckoning me. I know I'm not alone. We often don't know what needs to happen or how we will get there. And yet when we find our center in stillness, we remember that we have access to everything, and invariably, it is even more than we need.

This book has been a meditation in surrender. Listening. Trusting. And then surrendering more.

I am grateful to all who have shared their dreams and tears. To clients past and present, loved ones here and on the other side, and to all those who have shared dreams and tears, all who have entrusted me with their hearts and souls.

Victoria Maizes, thank you for captivating and inducting me into the raw elegance of Primal relationships. Kathleen McQuiggan and Pearl, I so value our early morning walks and your wisdom. Ann Marie Chaisson, thank you for finding what is right amid. Ryan, thank you for bringing creative wit, deep turns, and your discerning ear. Mom, for inspiring my persistence. Alishia, for sweating beside me, breathing with me, and being my beach. MeiMei, Jen, Cynthia, Rebecca, and Geoff, thank you for believing in me, the possibility, and the crazy timeline...

Thank you, Sheri, for cracking the door. Diane Danielson, for your timely, savvy guidance, Andrew Smith for inspiring me to speak from a more true space. Ivy Ross, for pushing boundaries. Mary Pat Ryan and Bill Courville, for constant nourishment and unconditional love. For our PowMow community and Eph Crew that keep it Real, playing full out and hollering through the Aspens. For family, who loved us fiercely through our grief (Jen and Ben, Laura and Doug, Phil and Erika), and Kevin, who stepped in and up with designs!

While I miss Phil and my Dad daily, I'm grateful for all who carry forward their spirit through their actions.

Candice Van Dertholen, for your profound presence, partnership in this work, and for amplifying (and repeating) what I wasn't yet ready or able to hear.

And Mark Newhall, thank you for leading from love and for the many times you stepped in to help guide this book forward.

About the Author

Camille Preston, Ph.D., is a business psychologist, executive coach, and leadership advisor with over two decades of experience guiding high-performing leaders through their most defining moments—grief, reinvention, expansion, and everything in between. She is the founder of AIM Leadership, a trusted partner to mission-driven leaders and organizations seeking clarity, courage, and meaningful impact in their work and lives.

Known for her rare blend of psychological insight, strategic vision, and deep compassion, Camille brings both research-based knowledge and lived experience to every conversation. What sets her apart isn't just what she knows—it's how she sees. Whether through keynotes, offsites, or coaching, Camille engages people in what truly matters by facilitating new ways of thinking, collaborating, leading, and living.

Camille invites her clients to lead from the inside out, with more honesty and less rigidity—to live, work, and lead with fewer regrets. Her third book, *Living Real*, is a deeply personal offering, born from a season of profound loss and inspired by the courageous stories of the many leaders she's walked beside. Through it, she offers more than insight—she extends an invitation: to be more human, more whole, and more present.

Camille lives in Cambridge, Massachusetts, with her husband and two children. When she's not writing or coaching, she's often running with friends, traveling light, or laughing her way through life's beautifully imperfect moments.

Connect with Camille—at www.AIMLeadership.com or info@AIMLeadership.com.

Appendix

Definitions

Activated

Feeling heightened engagement and focus, often as a result of a high-stress, high-pressure, high-stakes scenario. Cognitively engaged "logically" yet disconnected, frequently fueled by adrenaline and cortisol.

Altitude

The capacity to shift perspective to see differently. A mindset and skillset that helps us adapt to see either the bigger picture or the details while staying rooted in the moment.

Basement

The space that holds "bad or hard emotions." Feelings that are hard, uncomfortable, or that we don't like. Experiences we don't know how to feel or process. Examples include:

grief with no words, rage with no outlet, sadness that feels bottomless, fear that contracts us.

Containers

Intentional structures that support our ability to be fully present, to feel deeply, to open into the best version of ourselves. Such boundaries or systems can be beliefs, practices, or tools that help us experience the full range of life, supporting us in our authentic connection with ourselves and with others.

Enlivened

Energy that comes from being integrated, aligned, and impactful. A feeling of focused engagement as a result of full presence and connection. Openness to complexity, the unknown, and growth. Often experienced in flow.

First Floor

The face we present to the world. Where we live day-to-day—the part of us that we show others. It's our habits, expressions, and ways of showing up, which are not necessarily fake, but often filtered.

Impostor Syndrome

Feelings of self-doubt, incompetence, lack of achievement, combined with a fear of others perceiving you as a fraud (despite evidence of accomplishments and competence). A sense that I do not belong or deserve to be here.

Individuation
The lifelong process of becoming more fully yourself. The integration and acceptance of yourself (especially unconscious or Shallowed aspects) and your experiences into a more whole, balanced, and authentic self. It is often associated with separating from your family of origin.

Instagram Life
The external identity we project, regardless of whether or not we are on social media. The carefully curated image we share rather than the truth we live. The highlight reel we show others is polished, pretty, and often performative. It is solely the good, skips the messy parts, and hides what's Real.

Numbing
The ways we disconnect from emotions that feel too much. How we learned to mute vulnerability, avoid uncertainty, or escape discomfort. Often unconscious, it can reduce or shield us from pain... but also from presence.

Real Intelligence

RQ is awareness about what is and our capacity to be. It is not about managing emotions into neat, digestible boxes. It is about honoring them as data, as direction, as doorways to deeper integration.

Realing

Being present and engaged in the full range of life. Being with and embracing all of what is—the raw, genuine, unfiltered. Feeling fully what is, in that moment, standing inside the ache, the joy, the not-yet-knowing, without Shallowing, negating, or numbing emotions away.

Second Floor

Where we experience our lighter, more pleasant emotions, like joy, satisfaction, peace, fulfillment. The spaces we wish we experienced more, when we feel "okay," or even "great," as things feel aligned, open, and flowing.

Shallowing

The subtle, unconscious ways we mute feelings, narrow our existence, and limit emotions. How we avoid hard feelings and, in turn, unknowingly restrict our ability to feel joy, happiness, and fulfillment.

Sine Wave

The natural highs and lows of living. The arc of emotion, energy, and experience. Realing is about experiencing the full range of our individual Sine wave. It's not a problem to fix—it's the pulse of being human.

Soul Dysmorphia

When one's external world is misaligned or discordant with one's internal beliefs, values or aspiration. Characterized by excessive attention or preoccupation with external image or perception at the expense of their internal well-being.

To Real

To be present and engaged in the full range of life. To see things as they are, to stay present in the both/and, and to feel fully the raw, unfiltered, and authentic. To resist the urge to Shallow, numb, or dismiss challenging experiences.

www.ingramcontent.com/pod-product-compliance
Lightning Source LLC
Chambersburg PA
CBHW012252300426
44110CB00040B/2592